PEOPLE EMPOWERMENT

Achieving Success from Involvement

PEOPLE

EmPOWERMENT

Achieving Success from Involvement

Michael W. Gozzo

Wayne L. Douchkoff

PT Publications, Inc.
4360 North Lake Blvd.
Palm Beach Gardens, FL 33410
(407) 624-0455

591447

Library of Congress Cataloging in Publication Data

Gozzo, Michael W., 1939-
People empowerment: achieving success from involvement
        /Michael W. Gozzo, Wayne L. Douchkoff.
                p.   cm.
        Includes bibliographical references (p.   ) and index.
        ISBN 0-945456-07-7
        1. Work groups. 2. Problem solving. 3. Organizational
effectiveness.
I. Douchkoff, Wayne L., 1951-   II. Title.
HD66.G69   1992   92-4196
658.4'02--dc20   CIP

TABLE OF CONTENTS

PROFESSIONAL TEXTBOOKS

Available through PT Publications, Inc.
4360 North Lake Blvd.
Palm Beach Gardens, FL 33410

MADE IN AMERICA: *The Total Business Concept*
Peter L. Grieco, Jr. and Michael W. Gozzo

JUST-IN-TIME PURCHASING: *In Pursuit of Excellence*
Peter L. Grieco, Jr., Michael W. Gozzo and Jerry W. Claunch

SUPPLIER CERTIFICATION: *Achieving Excellence*
Peter L. Grieco, Jr., Michael W. Gozzo and Jerry W. Claunch

BEHIND BARS: *Bar Coding Principles and Applications*
Peter L. Grieco, Jr., Michael W. Gozzo and C.J. (Chip) Long

SET-UP REDUCTION: *Saving Dollars with Common Sense*
Jerry W. Claunch and Philip D. Stang

WORLD CLASS: *Measuring Its Achievement*
Peter L. Grieco, Jr.

THE WORLD OF NEGOTIATIONS: *Never Being a Loser*
Peter L. Grieco, Jr. and Paul G. Hine

VIDEO EDUCATION SERIES

SUPPLIER CERTIFICATION: *The Path to Excellence*
A nine-tape series on World Class Supplier Based Management

This book is dedicated to all those people
who responded when given the opportunity
to participate. Their dedication, perseverance
and the resulting performance stand as proof
that *we* can accomplish more than *I*.
A significant "we" that aided me with understanding
and constructive, thought-provoking statements
was my wife and friend, Deb. Thank you
for all your love and consideration
in all that happened during the writing of the book.

Mike

There are also people I would like to thank:
To the people I have worked for, with and
especially those who worked for me
and never ceased to impress me, themselves or
others with their accomplishments.
To my parents who put manufacturing in my blood
via the family business and taught me to strive
for continuous improvement.
To my children, Danielle and Shavonne,
for their loving support and encouragement,
especially during the trying times.
But especially to my wife, Marie, whom I admire
and am totally devoted to, for her patience,
tolerance and her words of encouragement
that helped me with the "words."

Wayne

PREFACE

The world's most potent and powerful resource — the human mind — is center stage once again.

But, that resource cannot be tapped without empowering people through their involvement in autonomous teams with a clear mission.

It is the purpose of **People Empowerment: Achieving Success from Involvement** to show you how to build teams, maintain their continued usefulness and unleash their full capacity in the business world of today and, more importantly, for tomorrow.

This book is based on the fact that it will be the human mind that will take ideas like Just-In-Time (JIT), Set-Up Reduction, Supplier Certification and Total Quality Control (TQC) and unlock their full potential. By using the mind, we are not limiting ourselves to executives and managers. We mean all the people who work in a company.

People Empowerment describes a process of encouraging participation through people involvement/empowerment. In this process, people are considered the primary resource for furthering productivity. Employees are encouraged to take the initiative in identifying problems and proposing solutions. Through participation in teams, people at all levels offer their unique expertise in a cooperative, problem solving process.

Why is People Involvement/Empowerment Necessary?

There is a one-word answer to that question. That word is *competition*. We need to empower people in order to unleash all the latent talent locked up in our work force. They are the ones who will pull us out of the competitive crisis into a posture of successful employment of our resources.

Both management and direct labor must come to realize that all of the people are a potential resource in solving problems. Whether the problem is cost-cutting or improving quality, everyone is on the "front lines" and they all have three characteristics which make their input not only valuable, but essential:

- They have the technical and/or historical background to understand how the problem affects their work.

- They are familiar with other people affected by the problem and the intricacies of the interpersonal relationships involved.

- They have a vested interest in coming up with a solution and making it work. Their job security in a global marketplace often depends upon their ingenuity.

We believe that all companies can benefit from a people involvement/empowerment program. In fact, the most recent research shows that significant results can be achieved in all sectors of our economy — manufacturing, service and professional. Given the economic climate and the continuing presence of a global marketplace, we owe it to ourselves to become more competitive by unleashing all the latent talent locked up in our work force.

Our Focus

People Empowerment will focus on how to energize the "critical mass" of employees to effect the culture change necessary to be competitive. We will map out how to acquire the necessary skills for survival in an increasingly competitive marketplace through allowing people to maximize their ability to solve problems. The emphasis will be on planning for the transition, developing the necessary skills, conducting effective team meetings and evaluating the results.

Michael W. Gozzo
Wayne L. Douchkoff

West Palm Beach, FL

ACKNOWLEDGMENTS

We would like to thank all of our clients for their good ideas, common sense and courage which was used to strive for continuous improvement. This book is their story of meeting one of America's most serious challenges. Special thanks go out to all of our colleagues at Pro-Tech who have challenged us and contributed their stories to this book. We thank them all for the time they took to review each chapter and make suggestions.

Special mention goes to Phil Stang who, besides offering editorial assistance, drew the illustrations in this book. We thank him for his accurate representations in support of people empowerment.

A special mention is also reserved for the capable and hard-working office staff who are always there for us as we travel across the country and even to foreign countries. Much appreciation is due to Steven Marks for his creative editorial assistance. We wish also to thank Kevin Grieco for his design of our book cover.

What we are most proud of is the sense of teamwork which exists at Pro-Tech. We see that people involvement/empowerment really works, each and every day. We hope this book will inspire you to achieve the same sense of commitment from your people.

PEOPLE EMPOWERMENT

Achieving Success from Involvement

Chapter One

MANAGEMENT
IN
PERSPECTIVE

MANAGEMENT
IN
PERSPECTIVE

The importance of the people who work in our businesses has taken center stage once again. While we have busied ourselves over the recent years with trotting out new technological advancements and management philosophies, our most valuable resource has been sitting unused in the wings. This is not to say the new technologies and ideas have been worthless. On the contrary, they were the opening acts to the main event, the drama in which you and I utilize the world's most potent and powerful resource—the human mind.

It is the human mind that will take ideas like Just-In-Time (JIT), Set-Up Reduction, Supplier Certification and Total Quality Control (TQC) and unlock their full potential. And that mind is not limited to only the thoughts and actions of executives and managers. The mind of which we speak encompasses all the people who work in a company. But, that resource cannot be tapped without empowering people through their involvement in autonomous teams with a clear mission. It is the purpose of our book to show you how to build teams, maintain their continued usefulness and unleash their full capacity in the business environment of today and, more importantly, of tomorrow.

Why should management engage in a program of people involvement and empowerment? Below are some of the more critical reasons:

- To build a stronger and more effective problem solving foundation.
- To develop skills in group dynamics.
- To improve communications.
- To improve a company's competitive edge through the use of the team approach.
- To encourage cooperation between labor and management.
- To establish an open door and open mind concept for doing business.
- To help all people in a company to become more effective listeners.
- To manage interpersonal conflicts and foster job satisfaction.
- To identify problems and recommend solutions in order to eliminate organizational waste and/or non-value added activities.
- To manage time effectively and avoid common pitfalls.
- To chart areas of change and opportunity.
- To break down visible and invisible barriers.
- To pave the way to the Total Business Concept (TBC) through people involvement/ empowerment.
- To develop a systematic approach and plan to implement change.
- To learn how to become a company's change agent in order to activate the potential of its people.

- To learn how to set up cross-functional teams which take a broad, rather than narrow, view of problems.
- To focus on Total Cost objectives for the entire organization.
- To elevate suppliers from victims to partners on the team.

As can be seen from this rather lengthy list of benefits, the question above may have been better phrased as "Why hasn't management taken advantage of so powerful and obvious a resource as the people who work in their own company?"

This book answers that question and many more by describing a process of encouraging participation through people involvement/empowerment. In this process, people are considered the primary resource for furthering productivity. Employees are encouraged to take the initiative in identifying problems and proposing solutions. Through participation in teams, people at all levels offer their unique expertise in a cooperative, problem solving process.

People involvement/empowerment can be viewed as a spectrum like the one on the next page which ranges from 1 to 10. Suggestion programs on the left side begin at 3 and self-governing work teams on the extreme right side rate a 10. Teams of people who develop solutions and then ask management for approval would rate a 6 on this spectrum.

Management should work toward moving their company to the right of this spectrum. Whether attaining 10 or not, you should realize that improvements will occur as you move along the spectrum.

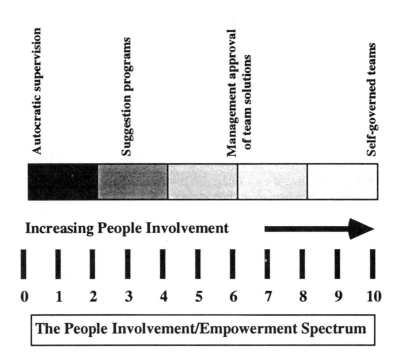

The People Involvement/Empowerment Spectrum

THE POWER OF PEOPLE INVOLVEMENT/EMPOWERMENT

Many companies have discovered the power of using the minds of their people. One company in Connecticut, which manufactures an engine retardant that works along with the service brake to assist in slowing down trucks, found out just how powerful. For years, the company operated in a traditional top-down fashion. They had little fear of competition because their product was protected by a patent. When the patent expired, however, the market quickly opened up to new competition and the Connecticut company was forced to find ways to cut costs in order to come up with a competitive price for their product.

Both JIT and TQC programs were identified as necessary concepts by the company in order to focus attention on quality and the elimination of waste. This was accomplished by educating employees about their role in the quality of the finished product and by training employees to build it right the first time. The manufacturing process, itself, was scrutinized for opportunities to increase productivity through the reduction of unnecessary and wasteful activities.

But, to make a long story short, the key to success was this company's empowerment of its people. The company looked upon problems as opportunities for improvement and people as the most potent resource for finding ways to improve. People at all levels of the company were encouraged to identify problems and propose solutions in an environment of teamwork. Within eighteen months, the company was beginning to realize the following significant improvements:

- Reduced product development cycles.
- Increased sales revenues (by 19%) as well as productivity gains.
- Reduced scrap and rework rates (by 68%).

The Bendix Friction Materials Division of Allied Signal is another company that found the power in people involvement/ empowerment. Their accomplishments, which are explained in detail in Chapter Nine, match those of the company above. Furthermore, these results were obtained at multiple sites and in a union environment. Nobody seemed more surprised at what was possible than the people themselves. They overcame a significant amount of doubt in the program to reach the high standards they now achieve regularly.

AN OVERLOOKED AND UNDERUTILIZED RESOURCE

For too long, non-management personnel, the people who supervise and staff a company's operations, have been overlooked as a potential resource in solving problems. Traditional methods of running a business say that it is management's job to provide solutions and everybody else's job to implement them. Not surprisingly, this rigid system had been the cause of many problems of its own between management and labor. The result of this rift has been the almost complete absence of teamwork in most companies today. Of course, nobody is expecting American workers to devote their entire life to the good of the company. But, the situation we now have in companies is so divisive, it threatens our competitive ability and even survival. When we assess a company's readiness for change, we often hear employees talk about "them" with great animosity. They are talking about management, other departments and fellow workers. It makes us wonder who the competition really is! All too often, management is unwilling and, by now, unable to listen to the ideal candidates for the task of problem solving — the very people who work in their companies. Whether the problem is cost-cutting or improving quality, the people doing the day-to-day work on the "front lines" have three characteristics which make their input not only valuable, but essential:

- They have the technical and/or historical background to understand how the problem affects their work.

- They are familiar with other people affected by the problem and the intricacies of the interpersonal relationships involved.

- They have a vested interest in coming up with a solution and making it work. Their job security in a global marketplace often depends upon their ingenuity.

A SURVEY OF YOUR TEAM ACTIVITY

At this point, take a few minutes and fill in the data sheet below about your company's team building activity. It will help you keep in mind what you are doing compared to what other companies are doing. In addition, you can use the information as a baseline from which to measure future progress as you implement the ideas in this book. All improvement begins with knowing where you now stand. That reminds us of the old joke about not being able "to get there from here." You certainly won't "get there" if you don't know where "here" is.

TEAM BUILDING DATA SHEET

Company (or Division) _____

1. Type(s) of teams currently in use at the facility:

_____
_____
_____

2. Number of active teams at the facility: _____

3. Types of teams under consideration for development:

_____
_____
_____

4. List five opportunities that will help your effort:

_____

_____

_____

_____

_____

5. List five problems that will hinder your effort:
   (Hint: Think about the requirement for a culture change.)

_____

_____

_____

_____

_____

WHAT'S WRONG WITH MANAGEMENT TODAY?

Killing Creativity

Now that you know where you stand, let's see where most companies stand today on the team building issue. We regret to say that many stand on shaky ground. The prevailing corporate culture of today is not conducive to the creative leadership needed to sow the seeds of people involvement/empowerment. Teresa Amabile, who studies creativity at Brandeis University, has identified five creativity killers:

> 1. Preventing people from selecting their own methods for doing a job or finding solutions to problems.

2. Creating an environment in which people feel as though they are constantly being watched.

3. Encouraging competition between people within a department or other such group.

4. Focusing on annual ratings as the most important performance criteria.

5. Using external rewards exclusively as a means to entice people to perform better.

Amabile points out that rewards and bonuses often have the effect of encouraging people to play it safe. In other words, the ability to make mistakes which opens the door to innovation is crushed by a conservative mind-set which closes the door on any improvement. (*TEI Newsletter*, December 1989/January 1990; p. 11.)

The Trust Gap

Recently, *Fortune* ran a cover story on the growing gap between top management and the rest of the people in the company. This gap has widened, the article says, to the point where employees are no longer believing anything that management says. The perception is that management is out to line its own pockets and that it is paying lip service to the notion that we are all in this together. In a survey of "100,000 middle managers, supervisors, professionals, salespeople and technical, clerical and hourly workers of Fortune 500 companies in 1988," Opinion Research Corp. of Chicago found that "employees believed top management now was less willing to listen to their problems than five years earlier.

The groups also felt top management now accorded them less respect." (*Fortune*, "The Trust Gap," Alan Farnham, Dec. 4, 1989; p. 56.)

The article also points out that most workers don't believe that top management knows what it is doing because it can't articulate a clear, coherent company vision. The people "in the trenches" believe that management has walled itself off from reality. Running a company has become an exercise in manipulating paper and not in making a product or providing a service. It is hard for an employee in this environment to believe that management really understands. And furthermore, when top executives lament the fact that a $10 million profit won't go far living the life style they lead, then something has gone wrong with the values of our companies.

It should come as no surprise that employees are not racing to jump on the wagon when management asks for help, especially when these people are routinely and systematically ignored.

How Not to Cut Costs

One method which management has used to cut costs has had a detrimental effect on the morale of the people who work for the company. That method is euphemistically called "downsizing." In more honest days, we referred to it as firing or laying off. To put it briefly, management shot itself in the foot using this method. They may have cut costs at first, but, in almost every instance of which we know, cost crept right back up to previous levels. Why? There was no longer anybody around who knew how to solve the inevitable problems a company runs up against. And those that are left may not care to solve problems even when the threat of further downsizing affects their jobs. The lesson that was not learned was that the human mind is the most efficient and effective cost-cutter that has ever been devised. So, the next time you think about cutting jobs, think about the real costs of that action—a brain-power drain and a demoralized work force that is unwilling to help a company survive.

A COMPANY THAT DOES IT RIGHT

One of the best examples of a company that treats its people with the respect deserved is Herman Miller Inc., the office furniture maker. A recent profile of the company in *Fortune* shows why they are succeeding and how they have built "sturdy bridges between management and employees." (*Fortune*, "Hot Company, Warm Culture," Kenneth Labich, Feb. 27, 1989; p. 74.)

Herman Miller has fostered a climate of shared respect in which even tough times serve to draw the company's people closer together. This philosophy even extends to the issue of salary. At Herman Miller, the salary of the chief executive can't be more than 20 times the average earnings of a line worker. Other American companies are beginning to adopt this practice as well. Ben and Jerry's, the famous ice cream maker, limits the top pay to no more than 5 times the lowest level of pay. Such a practice definitely gives the message that management is concerned about the whole company and not just their personal bank accounts.

Herman Miller is a firm believer in the value of teams as evidenced by their adoption of a performance evaluation program known as the Scanlon plan in which people receive a quarterly bonus that is derived from various criteria, including suggestions for cutting costs. All of the people in the company are on a team where they participate in problem solving. Every six months, the team leader rates his or her people and is evaluated, in turn, by each of the people. It is a simple example of the old adage: What's good for the goose is good for the gander.

Chairman Max DePree has made it a point to consult his people and has let it be known that all of his managers are expected to do the same. Not all management personnel have been successful all of the time. In the *Fortune* article noted above, many executives and managers get frustrated at the length of time it takes to make a decision when all the affected parties must be consulted. Most, however, admit that the frustration is worth it when they see the final results—a company with a real team spirit that is willing to tackle any problem.

Loran, a manufacturer of audio cassettes, learned the lesson of patience when a team of people finally decided to help themselves instead of listening to the verbalizing of management. They did an analysis of a tool used in the manufacturing process and not only achieved a payback in six months, but increased productivity by 60 percent.

Cardolite Corporation, a chemical manufacturer in Newark, NJ, also had to wait two months for a people involvement/empowerment team to begin recycling byproduct. But, once they started, the company did not experience the usual letdown which occurred two weeks after a project began. People involvement/empowerment kept the team excited and interested throughout the period.

THE NEED FOR A CHANGE

Successful companies are those with a management that has not only embraced business philosophies supporting win/win agreements and conformance to customer requirements, but has vigorously searched for and tapped its workers' knowledge. Companies exist in an environment in which they must compete for survival. It makes sense to use every resource available.

Internal and External Forces for Change

In his book, **Change Agents,** Manuel London cites external and internal forces affecting business changes. The lists he constructs are based on the work done by two organizational development experts (Richard Beckhard and Reuben Harris) in 1977 as they predicted what the future held for business. The forces they noted have come true and are still true today. What is most interesting about the cited forces is that they are best met by a company which fosters a climate of people involvement/empowerment. Later in this chapter, we will look at an example of such a company. For now, let's list and explain the external and internal forces at work on your company today as noted by London in his book:

EXTERNAL FORCES

- Companies will need to respond to complex environments where many different constituencies will make their demands.

- The emphasis will shift from viewing the company as "producing wealth for its owners" to producing "wealth (employment) for society," London points out.

- College graduates just entering the business world will have increasingly high expectations and will move frequently to attain them.

- People in mid-career or at a middle level in the company will become more and more interested in the quality of life than career advancement.

- The growth of technology will slow down. "The human component of high creativity and motivation will be more important to competitive advantage than technological developments," says London.

- "Jobs at the lower levels of a company will have low expectations," says London. They will not be easily motivated to help a company improve quality or productivity.

INTERNAL FORCES

- Generalists will be better able to solve tomorrow's complex problems than specialists.

- Companies will need to improve the quality of life in the work environment and recognize that people also require time for a relatively stress-free life outside of work.

- Companies will need to find ways to help their people become more creative by using teams and more flexible organizational structures.

- Companies will need to spend more time on solving organizational problems and other change technologies that have to do with communication and group dynamics.

- Companies will need to grant authority and responsibility to all levels of the organization.

(**Change Agents**, Manuel London, Josey-Bass Publishers, San Francisco, 1988; p. 15-18.)

To be honest, not many companies are aware of the forces above and even fewer are doing anything about them. And, all too often, those that do make changes have done so because they have been forced to respond to crises. We know that there is a better way than being reactive. In fact, we see people involvement and empowerment as proactive. Companies able to use the minds, talents and skills of their people are the companies who will have prepared themselves for any eventuality in the future. One way to become more proactive is to start employing Just-In-Time (JIT) and Total Quality Control (TQC) in your company.

WHAT JIT AND TQC CAN DO

Good companies are able to apply the latest technologies in making their products or providing their service. What distinguishes a great company, however, is its ability to use this technology to conform to customer requirements. The best of these top echelon companies have discovered how to involve and empower their people through a business philosophy which places its emphasis on 100% quality and the elimination of all waste and wasteful activities in the entire organization. Such a business philosophy is JIT/TQC.

The essence of JIT/TQC is that every activity leading to the end product (or service) should be *done right the first time*. The goal is to make quality paramount in every decision related to satisfying the customer's requirements; and to make that goal attainable through involvement of cross-functional teams with the necessary funds, authority and responsibility. In addition, the JIT/TQC concept advocates that the timing of each activity in a process be such that activity #1 is not completed until activity #2 is ready. The goal here is avoid unnecessary delays between activities and to reduce inventory so that problems can be seen and corrected. This applies equally well to the inventory (i.e., backlog) of customer orders being processed at order entry. The old system of manufacturing depends on huge inventories to cover up inefficiencies. They act as buffers, a Just-in-Case mentality. We all, of course, pay for these huge inventories in higher product cost and poor quality. JIT/TQC, on the other hand, employs a pull system in which batches of one are strived for and where replenishment of inventory is only triggered by customer demand.

For many companies, the undertaking of JIT/TQC has resulted in the following benefits:

- Reduced lead-times.
- Reduced defect rates.
- Reduced total cost.
- Reduced set-up times.
- Increased on-time delivery.
- Increased productivity.
- Stable work force.
- Higher morale.

The above benefits are the easily quantifiable ones. In our experience, the hidden benefits far outweigh the ones above or are responsible for the results above. We're talking about the intangible sense of teamwork that is present in every properly run JIT/TQC implementation. People pull for each other, stimulate coworker's ideas, find low cost, common sense solutions to nagging problems, and so on. The list is endless. As long as companies are faced with competition, the sparks of imagination which occur at JIT/TQC team meetings will insure that the list always remains endless. Using a team philosophy is like working in one of the top laboratories in the world where the people are on the leading edge of innovation. We aren't exaggerating when we say that people involvement and empowerment is the wave of the future. It is one of the keys to business survival.

HOW TO MAKE THE TRANSITION TO TBC

TBC, or the Total Business Concept seeks to eliminate all waste from a company and to strive for continuous improvement in order to make a World Class company. Education and training will be the foundation of your transition to being a World Class company. This will be done in two areas.

One, a company will need to develop programs in which managers will learn how to manage change effectively. This, indeed, is one of the principal reasons behind the writing of this book. Management has to be alerted to the consequences of failing to act on people involvement/empowerment and subsequently losing the benefits which could have been accrued.

Two, a company will need to develop orientation programs for all levels of the organization. The goal should be that every person in the company can tell you what JIT/TQC is, how it works and what their role is. This effort will require the service of a number of cross-functional teams composed of people from the affected disciplines. Many companies have also used their human resource department as an internal consultant to these and other teams. Other companies have found more satisfying results by hiring outside consultants.

Along with education and training, a company must show its commitment by allocating funds. Sounds obvious, but we've seen too many companies who didn't back up their words with cold, hard cash. When costs are compared with benefits, it is readily apparent that this is a cost justified investment. Another necessary ingredient for making the transition is to draw up a list of long-term and short-term objectives. This list should not be written by management alone, but with the consultation of people at all levels of the company. After these objectives are listed, it is equally important to use your people to determine how the company's efforts will be evaluated and what types of rewards will be given for performance which matches or exceeds stated goals.

As can be seen, the successful transition is accomplished through a company-wide program. Three companies have been so successful in these types of programs that they have gone on to win the Malcolm Baldrige National Quality Award and Japan's prestigious Deming Award. Milliken & Company (a Baldrige winner), for example, has set up a number of self-managed teams and, in 1988, spent approximately $1,300 per employee for training. One of the results was the elimination of nearly 700 management positions.

Xerox (a Baldrige winner) has spent more than $125 million and 4 million work-hours on quality training. That comes out to about 27 hours per employee. More than 75 percent of the company's people are involved in at least one of 7,000 quality improvement teams. Florida Power and Light, the first American winner of the

Deming Award, has thousands of its employees on almost 2,000 teams which attack and solve problems.

ESTABLISHING A COHESIVE MANAGEMENT STYLE

Your management style is an important factor in establishing a receptive climate for change. Over the last few decades, the qualities that make up the ideal manager or executive have come under a great deal of scrutiny. In his book, **The Human Side of Enterprise** (1960), Douglas M. McGregor analyzed different management styles. Under his definition of Theory X, he suggested that most managers believe the average person does not like to work. A manager with this belief would motivate his subordinates through fear and close supervision. McGregor felt that this was an ineffective means of motivating people and created Theory Y as an alternative for boosting productivity. McGregor's Theory Y manager believed that people were motivated to achieve and to grow and that they would thus act responsibly in their jobs. The Theory Y manager motivated his subordinates by defining objectives for them to achieve.

In 1981, William G. Ouchi described yet another management style in his book, **Theory Z**. His approach suggested that people were the key to increased productivity. He advocated that the key to motivating people was to understand their values and treat them in accordance with that understanding. The goal was to manage people so that they could work together effectively and productively. Here, decision making was the result of cooperation and participation. This management style empowered all the people in the company in its effort to increase productivity.

The people involvement and empowerment process described in this book is compatible with Ouchi's Theory Z. The Theory Z person is the ideal candidate for establishing an environment in which all people in a company work together toward mutual goals. How, then, can you motivate people to buy into an environment where all employees participate in the decision-making process?

MOTIVATION

Ouchi and many others have discovered that the key to higher productivity and improved quality is an individual's attitude toward his or her work. The best way to get people to respect their work is to respect them. It's as old-fashioned as the Golden Rule: Do unto others as you would have them do unto you. That means you have to respect their internal needs and desires which may or may not relate to the work they do at the company. Managers need to realize that one of the primary motivators for an employee is the ability to enjoy the fruits of his or her labor when he or she leaves work for the day, weekend or vacation.

External motivators, or those factors which are not part of the internal psychological make-up of a person, are also important for a company to consider. Perhaps the most important external factor is the corporate culture. Does your company have a clear vision of where it is going and how it is going to get there? Does it give its people the responsibility and authority to meet challenges in a manner most fitting to a team's needs? The answers to these questions will require a company to continuously balance the desires of individuals for autonomy with an equally strong desire for people to be part of some group engaged in a meaningful endeavor. That's not easy, but it's absolutely necessary in today's business climate.

Companies will need to establish a new internal culture that encourages people involvement/empowerment. They will have to foster an inquisitive climate where problems are solved by listening to the ideas of people and then acquiring the resources which will allow the people to get the job done. We're reminded of a story told by a participant at one of our seminars. He is now a supervisor, but had worked on the line for a number of years before his promotion. As a line worker, he kept informing management that if they would buy him a certain tool, he could do his job faster and more accurately. Ten years went by and no tool was forthcoming. Then, as a supervisor, he made the same request. The tool was bought and used. An investment of approximately $25 literally saved thousands. Think how much more could have been saved if the company had a culture of listening to its people ten years ago!

WHAT NEEDS TO HAPPEN—REQUIRED CHANGES

To summarize what we have said so far, the following changes must be made by companies in order for them to make the transition to a people-powered company:

> **Attitude Change**—Management must see the people working for a company as a valuable resource which should be consulted and informed.
>
> **Culture Change**—The company must adopt proactive rather than reactive management philosophies and create an atmosphere of trust where people are empowered and involved.

A new organizational culture is required in order to facilitate the changes necessary for the future. The culture must be one in which people feel free to take the initiative in approaching upper management with problems and ideas for solving them. An "open-ear" policy is an integral part of this new environment. We say "open-ear" because an "open-door" policy often doesn't have the desired result of producing a policy of listening. In fact, the eventual outcome of this new culture of which we speak is to have teams which are self-governing. Such teams don't need to walk through management's door for authority to solve problems. They should have been given that mandate long ago. Management's primary job in the future is to be an internal "consultant" who helps to facilitate change.

It will probably be necessary to evaluate present organizational structures in order to promote this policy. People need to feel that management has given them the authority, responsibility and resources to put their ideas into action. Even physical barriers which emphasize status such as office size and location must be reconsidered. Managers and engineers will need to sit on the factory floor in order to encourage more direct involvement. Traditional dress codes may have to go the way of the buggy whip. The list of things which need changing is different for each company, but the changes cited here and in other places in this book are typical of all businesses.

The illustration on the next page gives you a clear idea of what we are discussing. Specifically, the graph shows how a team gains responsibility and authority as management releases control.

SEVEN RULES FOR SUCCESS

The transition to people involvement/empowerment is one that affects the entire company. Every thought and every action must be revised to accommodate the effort toward improving quality

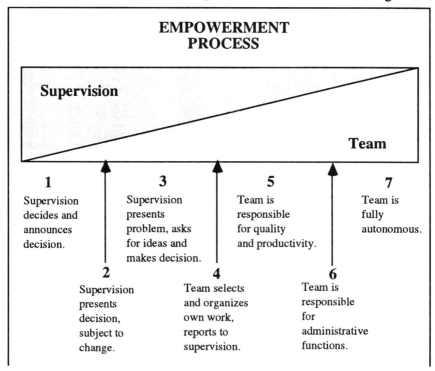

EMPOWERMENT PROCESS

Supervision

Team

1
Supervision
decides and
announces
decision.

2
Supervision
presents
decision,
subject to
change.

3
Supervision
presents
problem, asks
for ideas and
makes decision.

4
Team selects
and organizes
own work,
reports to
supervision.

5
Team is
responsible
for quality
and productivity.

6
Team is
responsible
for
administrative
functions.

7
Team is
fully
autonomous.

and productivity. The business of business has been traditionally
planned and supervised by management. Managers defined long-
and short-term goals. The difficulty with this method of managing
is that it is imposed from above. People are not going to roll out
the welcome mat for this kind of management. In order to realize
success, there must be a plan to gain the commitment of people.
The following rules for success are the focal points in the transition to people involvement/empowerment.

1. **Make quality a top priority.** It isn't
    enough to say that quality is a corporate
    priority. It must be evident in every deci-
    sion and every action taken by a company.
    Quality must become a way of life.

2. **Eliminate unnecessary activities.** This
will necessitate that everybody in a
company take a closer look at the way
things are getting done and ask "Why?"
And then ask "Why?" again. And again.
And again until improvements are made
in company operations. Some questions
to ask: Why does the process work this
way? Are there steps that could be performed more efficiently? Or, better yet,
are there steps in the process that could
be eliminated altogether?

Consider the time involved in obtaining
approvals prior to a purchase taking
place. Even though a purchase may be
small in amount, it often requires the
review and signatures of several layers of
management. Perhaps a work team can
find a way to condense this process.
Pushing the decision down to the user
level expedites the procedure and creates
time for solving other problems.

3. **Empower people.** The first step is to
view people as resources. Then identify
ways for them to use their skills and
brainpower for maximum effectiveness.
In addition, do the following:

- Give workers the resources and authority to do their jobs.

- Encourage teamwork and team-based decisions.

- Establish methods for self-monitoring work progress.

- Give people the authority to do whatever it takes to get the job done.

4. **Discover new ways to communicate.** In a process driven by employees, effective internal communications become increasingly significant. Throughout the organization, people must be educated in the "how-to's" of the people involvement/ empowerment process. After the initial training, a new way of thinking must become part of an on-going corporate language that everybody understands. In addition to understanding the process, people will need to be kept abreast of corporate progress. Why not share the financial results of each quarter with your people? They will gain a better understanding of the challenge of survival and corporate positioning in a competitive market.

5. **Look outside the boundaries.** A familiar puzzle asks the challenger to find a way to connect all the dots in the figure on the next page:

The following rules must be observed:

- Use no more than 4 straight lines to connect the dots.
- The 4 lines must be connected (i.e., drawn without lifting the pencil).

Many challengers would place all their focus on attempting to find a solution that would fit within the boundaries created by the nine dots and thus limit the possible solutions to the problem. The solution, of course, lies in considering the space outside the boundaries.

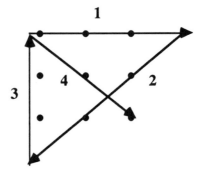

Begin to question why things are done the way they are done. Advanced technolo-

gies are not the only alternative for improving productivity. Discover more
options by finding new ways to look at the
same old problems.

**(For more excellent examples of how teams solve
problems, look at the case studies in Chapter Nine.)**

   6.   **Offer plenty of support.** As people
        begin to take on new responsibilities
        related to the empowerment and involve-
        ment process (such as attending team
        problem solving meetings and monitoring
        progress), they need to know they have
        support. Offering paid team meeting time
        and replacement cadre for breaks and
        personal time are just a couple of ways to
        encourage the transition to the new way.

   7.   **Establish quantitative measurements.**
        Your people won't know where they are
        headed if there isn't some type of meas-
        urement program in place. This program
        should establish a baseline (the point
        where you begin) and milestones to be
        achieved in your company's progress in
        attaining the goals of improved quality
        and greater productivity.

Why is People Involvement/Empowerment Necessary?

There is a one-word answer to the question which heads this
section. That word is *competition*. We need to empower people in

order to unleash all the latent talent locked up in our work force. They are the ones who will pull us out of the competitive crisis in which we find ourselves. And a crisis it is! According to a recent story in the **Wall Street Journal**, the Big Three auto makers still trail Japanese auto makers by a considerable margin in quality. In fact, the Japanese have increased their quality lead over American autos. The reason? American autos didn't get worse; in fact, they got considerably better. But the Japanese autos were made even better than that. They used their people to gain the competitive edge. We can, too, but it's quite obvious that we need to address the very serious issues listed below:

- Customer/Supplier Relationships.
- Return on Investment.
- World Competition.
- Market Share.
- Eroding Profit.
- No Long-Term Objectives.
- High Inventory.
- Internal Waste.

When we look at these issues, we **must not** come up with traditional answers. In the past, if a company's profit picture started to erode, the normal reaction was to cut people. Today, that solves nothing over the long run. The very real problems above are not addressed by simply downsizing, laying off or firing. The people you lose are, in fact, the only people who can help the company sail out of its doldrums.

Japanese management experts who look at our problem agree with what we have been telling our clients for years. The major cause of all our problems is that management blames everything and everybody except itself for the present predicament. And employees are the principal group that gets the blame. This is completely counterproductive. The Japanese see this blaming as irrational at best and suicidal at worst. They cannot understand why we don't listen to, even demean, our most powerful resource.

MAKING A LONG-TERM COMMITMENT

In order to meet both domestic and foreign competition with a people involvement/empowerment process that addresses the issues above, there is one more absolutely vital requirement—a long-term commitment to the process. There are several factors in making a long-term commitment. Management must realize that results will not be immediate and that the people in a company will need time to overcome a skepticism which is the result of years of being uninvolved.

In the people involvement/empowerment process, people will be asked to work together in a new way. It may take time for them to develop skills which will allow them to interact effectively. It will take time for them to believe that this is not just another management fad. An understanding of this is essential if we are to manage the change process.

Management must also realize that actions are far more effective than words in convincing people that a long-term commitment is being made. Finding ways to communicate through a more inclusive and open method will be one of the first steps made toward opening the doors and ears of management to the ideas of people.

The bulletin on the following pages, which was circulated at our client, General Foods, will show you just how powerful people involvement/empowerment can be:

GENERAL FOODS BULLETIN

As many of you are aware, the plant JIT Steering Committee has been conducting a contest to change the name "J.I.T." There was a need for a name change because many people from outside the plant thought that "J.I.T." was an inventory reduction program. As we all know, J.I.T. is more than an inventory reduction program.

It is a:

"Methodology by which we use the entire work force to eliminate waste."

However, as hard as we all tried, we could not convey this definition to everyone. Therefore, we used the problem solving techniques we learned as part of our JIT training and decided that a name change was necessary.

The response to the contest was overwhelming with many great suggestions. In fact, there were so many great suggestions that picking one winner was impossible. Therefore, we combined the best of all the responses to come up with:

Quality
Utilizing
Employee
Support
Teams

A Journey to Excellence

Thank you for all your effort in the Dover J.I.T. program.

It is now time to <u>continue</u> our **Q.U.E.S.T.**

Q.U.E.S.T. Steering Committee

OUR FOCUS

The remainder of this book will focus on how to energize the "critical mass" of employees to effect the culture change necessary to be competitive. We will map out how to acquire the necessary skills for survival in an increasingly competitive marketplace by allowing people to maximize their ability to solve problems. The emphasis will be on planning for the transition, developing the necessary skills, conducting effective team meetings and evaluating the results.

But for now, we leave you with a list of questions to ponder and which will be answered in this book:

- How do you mix different types of skills and expertise on work teams?

- How can you introduce greater flexibility in work schedules and staffing?

- How can you use new technologies to enhance flexible arrangements which improve the quality of the product or service and the effectiveness of people.

- How can you develop teams which are capable of effective self-management?

- How will you integrate a number of different management styles needed at various stages into one coherent strategy?

- How can you help teams work on reducing total cost?

- How can you keep up with the trend toward more education and training?

- How will you maintain morale and commitment during times of transition?

- How will you prepare management for coming changes?

- How can you use surveys to assess people's needs and attitudes?

In the next chapter, we will look at how to get a program of people involvement/empowerment started. In particular, we will discuss the issues of leadership and motivation as a way to prepare the company for the change process. Underlining all of this will be a look at how to survey your organization in order to gain a sense of where to start.

Chapter Two

GETTING STARTED:

PLANNING, DIRECTING, DELEGATING

GETTING STARTED:

PLANNING, DIRECTING, DELEGATING

A process of people involvement/empowerment provides a path to a future of numerous opportunities. However, before companies can pass through the gate (see next page) which separates the staid business environment of the past from the innovative environment of the future, they must prepare for their journey just as any exploration team would. Simply knowing what you want to see on the other side is not enough. That's like saying you know you want to go to Europe to see the Eiffel Tower, Stonehenge and the Sistine Chapel during April of next year and then failing to book your flights. You should know by now that a process of people involvement/empowerment will help your company in its quest for the following:

- A stronger and more effective problem solving foundation.

The Gate from the Past to the Future

- A network of improved communication.

- Numerous teams with highly developed skills in group dynamics.

- An environment safe for constructive disagreement.

- A finely honed competitive edge.

- An increased variety of perspectives.

- A greater pool of resources.

- A more egalitarian workplace.

But, knowledge of the goals of this quest is not enough to insure success, let alone implement a process. Your company must incorporate them into its culture and recognize that it is never too late to begin addressing these issues.

Care should be taken not to expect early results. Success comes to those companies which move patiently, but persistently through the people involvement/empowerment process. You need to set and then strive for realistic objectives that each and every team can understand and achieve. Most important of all, you absolutely must provide your teams with support in the form of people and resources. And finally, employees need to understand that a people involvement/empowerment process works to enhance business and eventually their security.

The following short survey will give you some idea of where your company stands on the issues which are needed to get a people involvement/empowerment process started. Take time right now to appraise your company and see what this survey indicates about your company's needs.

GETTING STARTED SURVEY

For each category on the following pages, circle the number which best indicates how you feel about your company's level of people involvement and empowerment.

1 - Disagree strongly.   4 - Agree.
2 - Disagree.   5 - Strongly agree.
3 - Not sure.

1. Communications: Transfer of information   1 2 3 4 5
between senior management and other levels
in our organization is effective.

2. Leadership: Senior management employs a   1 2 3 4 5
participative philosophy to reach its goals.

3. Decision Making: The organization solves   1 2 3 4 5
problems and makes decisions which are
appropriate to the situation.

4. Cooperation: All levels of the company have   1 2 3 4 5
strong levels of coordination and cooperation.

5. Planning: The ability to set realistic goals and   1 2 3 4 5
develop plans encourages people involvement
and empowerment.

6. Responsiveness: Level of preparation for   1 2 3 4 5
unforeseen events is healthy.

7. Control: Guidance and feedback on actions   1 2 3 4 5
are provided in a positive way.

8. Motivation: Effective team performance and   1 2 3 4 5
morale are encouraged by senior management.

9. Conflict: Conflicts are resolved in a positive   1 2 3 4 5
manner.

A score of 42 or above would seem to indicate that you are firmly wedded to people involvement/empowerment. Those few companies which are at this level do not, however, rest upon their laurels. They are out seeking even more education and training to raise their level even higher. People involvement/empowerment goes hand-in-hand with the Continuous Improvement Process (CIP). A score between 36 and 42 indicates that your company is well on its way to providing an environment where people involvement/ empowerment programs can flourish. Any score below 36 means that your company had better start understanding people empowerment or face competition which could jeopardize its survival.

If your company is like most, it needs to do some work in order to empower its people and increase its capacity to excel in the global marketplace. The work which your company faces begins with honest appraisals similar to the one you just completed. Assessment, in fact, is among the first items in the list below of important "getting started" factors:

"GETTING STARTED" FACTORS

1. Establishment of a vision, i.e., vision statement.

2. Assessment of the company and people in all functions and their readiness for people involvement/empowerment.

3. Establishment of a plan to accomplish the creation of a team environment.

4. Definition of short and long range objectives.

"GETTING STARTED" FACTORS
(continued)

5. Ownership and responsibility at the lowest level.

6. Definition of expectations and setting of goals.

7. Understanding of behavioral requirements of people and functions.

Exploration efforts require leadership and so does establishing a people involvement/empowerment process based on the factors above. But what kind of leadership? What skills should a leader possess? What makes a company a leader in innovative and flexible management?

LEADERSHIP CHARACTERISTICS

Foremost on the list of leadership characteristics which companies must have or implement is a process to develop people on a regular basis. Motorola, for example, has created Motorola University to meet the needs and demands both of the company and of the people who work there. In fact, this Baldrige award-winning company sees striving for continuous improvement through people participation as a way of life and survival. The leadership characteristics which we will discuss become part of the company's "personality."

Your company will need to foster people at all levels who have the following leadership skills (remember that in a participative environment of self-managed teams, all people are leaders):

ESSENTIAL SKILLS
FOR AN EFFECTIVE LEADER

A keen perception.
Compassion toward others.
A futuristic outlook.
Flexibility.
Focus.
A positive attitude.
Ability to listen.
Patience.
A desire to continually improve.

A keen perception. A leader develops a keen perception by learning to walk a mile in another person's shoes. As she looks at problems from the point of view of others, she is able to gain their unique insights into a problem. The added insight will assist a leader in guiding a team as it looks at problems in order to separate causes from symptoms, generates multiple costed solutions and chooses the solution most likely to produce the desired results.

Compassion toward others. An effective leader makes a sincere effort to be sensitive to the needs of others. Abraham Maslow, the psychologist famous for his hierarchy of human needs, begins his hierarchy at the level in which food and shelter are met and builds toward the highest level of need which he defined as "self-actualization," or the need for personal fulfillment. If a leader can help individuals realize self-actualization through a meaningful work experience, workers will be more interested and motivated to achieve. People are more likely to give their all when their needs are being met. A leader's sensitivity will become apparent through person to person communications, opportunities for people career development and efforts toward providing for an individual's future with a secure job.

A futuristic outlook. A leader must have a vision of the future. This is what will carry the company from the known to the unknown along a clearly defined path of people involvement/ empowerment. Such a leader realizes that management's true job is to provide vision and direction, not to dictate prescriptions and details. The company of the future will be more open, egalitarian and responsive to people's need for meaningful work.

Flexibility. Flexibility prepares a leader to be ready to manage change. It is his role in people involvement/empowerment to make sure that all employees of the company understand why flexibility in the workplace will allow the company to be more competitive in the marketplace. Flexibility must exist in the organizational structure and must be demonstrated via employment of problem solving techniques. Finally, flexibility must become part and parcel of a company's culture.

Focus. Focus is the quality a leader uses to help teams move toward defined goals. By keeping her eyes on the target, a leader slowly moves forward into the future, evolving in the process to a more desired state. The challenge of focusing in this manner lies in filtering out distractions. A leader must learn to separate those details that move the company closer to the target from those that cause the company to miss the bull's-eye.

A positive attitude. A leader shapes the attitude of people. His positive attitude is a model within the company which will breed confidence and foster a "can-do" attitude. Others will pick up on this aura and reflect what is being modeled. A positive attitude is contagious and an important part of a receptive culture. Without confidence, management of the change process is difficult.

At the same time, it is important to recognize a negative attitude. This situation requires counsel. Confronting this attitude with a compassionate ear will help identify the source of the problem so that corrective action can be taken immediately.

Ability to listen. In order for a leader to be sensitive, compassionate and perceptive, she must first be a good listener. By hearing and understanding what people have to say, a leader will gain valuable insight which will result in a greater awareness. Another bonus to be gained by the listener is an improvement in interpersonal relationships. People enjoy talking when they have an attentive audience. When a leader listens carefully to what is being said, the speaker walks away from the conversation feeling that he has participated in a valuable and important, two-way communication.

Leaders must open their ears to what people are saying in order to make full use of available resources. The tips that follow are useful for improving listening skills:

- Reserve judgment about what the speaker is saying. Place your focus on understanding what is being said.

- Learn to screen out distractions that affect your ability to focus on what the speaker is saying.

- Look for additional meaning in what is being said through clues the speaker gives, such as gestures or posture.

- As the speaker is talking, try to mentally summarize what is being said.

- Restate what was said in your own words to ensure understanding.

Patience. An effective leader must approach his vision of the future with patience. He must set aside the quick fixes in favor of a strategy that will have greater benefits over the long haul. However, there are times when quick action is necessary. The astute leader blends short- and long-term strategies.

A desire to continually improve. This is a state of mind that the most effective leaders all have. These people are not content with succeeding. They want to move on and top their previous performance. If their company reaches 99 percent on-time delivery, they immediately start a process to get the percentage up to 99.5 and when it reaches that level, they strive for 99.8 percent. With competition around the world being as intense as it is, we think that a company and its leaders can do no less than adopt this mental set.

CHARACTERISTICS OF LEADING COMPANIES

Now that you have learned about what is necessary for the individual as a leader, let's turn to an observation of the company as a whole. What characteristics should a company possess in order to be a leader in people involvement/empowerment? Rosabeth Moss Kanter, in her book **Change Masters**, distinguishes between "integrationist" and "segmentalist" companies. "Integrationists" are successful at using people involvement and empowerment programs to stimulate what we have called the innovative potential of people. Such companies are not afraid of departmental walls crumbling down. They are aware that a certain amount of chaos breeds creativity, an idea echoed by Tom Peters in his book, **Thriving On Chaos**. We have seen time and time again that people become involved and empowered when they are given full responsibility and authority to solve problems. We have also seen the "segmentalist" companies in which the organization is so rigid and highly structured that new ideas are crushed under the weight of bureaucracy. These are not the types of companies which allow people to seek meaningful work relationships. A certain amount of local autonomy and independence for teams of people is a necessary characteristic of a company which seeks to become a leader.

William G. Dyer, in his book **Team Building**, agrees that blurred distinctions between departments or functions are crucial to people involvement/empowerment. He goes on to cite several other factors which should be present in an organization in order for people involvement/empowerment to have the most success:

- An environment exists in which people can regularly meet as groups to discuss goals and problems.

- The organization is sufficiently adaptable to support informal exchanges of information and, in fact, encourages such channels.

- Interdependence between people and departments is encouraged.

- The company has a "fluid structure, few operating policies and procedures, and emerging role definitions." (**Team Building**, p. 163)

Leading companies which possess the characteristics described above are, of course, much more receptive to finding out where their areas of opportunity are located.

IDENTIFYING AREAS OF OPPORTUNITY

Leading companies, as we have already noted, are always striving to improve, always looking for places where they can get better. Building on what has been discussed so far, the overall process for implementing a people involvement/empowerment process takes the following four basic steps:

---

1. **Identify areas of opportunity.**
2. **Gather information through organizational surveys.**
3. **Structure the work force into teams.**
   - A. **Introduce group dynamic skills.**
   - B. **Teach problem solving skills.**
4. **Institute a performance measurement program and a feedback system.**

In this chapter, we will discuss the first two. Step three will be covered by Chapters Four through Seven and step four by Chapter Eight.

The entire process of people involvement/empowerment begins with the identification of an area or areas of opportunity. In effect, this is the same as implementing a Continuous Improvement Process at your company since identifying problems and opportunities begins with the desire for change. This desire for change is the result of observing the difference between the ideal and actual states of a process, product or service — missed delivery dates, inferior quality, excessive absenteeism and less obvious examples such as motivation, quality of life, attitude, ambition.

Whatever the area of opportunity, we firmly believe that it should be felt strongly by the people whose work will be affected by any changes. In other words, opportunity is not only what management sees as opportunity, but also what the people who work in the organization see as opportunity. When the need grows naturally out of the perceptions of people working the soil, so to speak, then there is a far greater chance that the participative process will take root and flourish.

To help you identify these areas of opportunity, we have listed several questions and frameworks which will guide you:

1. Ask yourself why:

- You can't get what you need when you need it.
- Tools, etc. are never where they should be.
- Results change every time you check a process.
- Processes or machines work at some plants and not yours.
- Excess inventory sits on the floor or in the warehouse.

**2. Look at the following list of symptoms
which indicate areas for improvement:**

- Decrease in production output.
- Increase in complaints from workers.
- Friction among workers.
- Number of union grievances.
- Confusion about direction of assignments.
- Incomplete assignments.
- No involvement from workers.
- More meetings and less results.
- Increase in customer complaints.
- Inability to meet deadlines.
- Increase in errors.
- Lack of efficiency due to outdated systems or
  procedures.
- Poor internal communications.
- Dumb mistakes where nobody is at fault.

**3. Observe variances between expected and
actual results in the following areas:**

- Quality.
- Cost reduction.
- Productivity and delivery.
- Preventive maintenance.
- Human resources.
- Profitability.

**4. Most symptoms — such as low productiv-
ity — are the consequence of two factors.
They are:**

- Differences between people and higher levels
of management which often manifest themselves as overconformity. This is doing
everything the boss says in order not to get in
trouble. We call this the "pain avoidance
syndrome." Other times, this type of difference will show up as passive resistance such
as "going exactly by the book" or coming in
five minutes late every day. Overt resistance
is demonstrated through strikes, work actions,
sick-outs, etc.

- Problems between people who work together
in a department, function or team. This can
also be passive or overt. The cause can best
be ascertained by listening closely to the
complaints of people.

**5. The following list of questions will help you
determine which area of opportunity
should be worked upon first:**

- What are the potential cost and benefits?
- How many people and how many resources
will be needed to address this area of opportunity?
- Do upper levels of management perceive the
need and recognize it as an opportunity for
improvement?
- What levels of the organization will be affected by addressing this area?
- In which department or function did the need
originate?

MANAGING THE BUSINESS

As a company initiates the participatory process, there soon comes a need to develop guidelines which will oversee the process. Foremost is the recognition that we require teams of people. The efforts required to build these teams break down into three phases:

```
DESIGN AND SURVEY
    PROCESS
   FOLLOW UP
```

In the first phase, **Design and Survey**, companies begin by interviewing and surveying people to search for the areas of opportunity noted above. Attitudes are important here. We will shortly discuss how to conduct an organizational survey. For now, however, all you need to know is that this phase provides the information which is necessary to formulate a plan for implementing the people involvement/empowerment process. In the second phase, the **Process** itself, team members are taught essential skills in team dynamics such as decision making, listening and communication, creativity and problem solving. In the third phase, team members devise ways of monitoring performance and keeping the Continuous Improvement Process working.

We believe that people involvement/empowerment programs should be self-directing, or autonomous. After all, individuals must ultimately be responsible for their own results. While teams of people are concentrating on fulfilling company objectives, management can spend their time on business applications and responding to competition. This won't be possible until management learns how to share responsibility and authority through all levels. The organization exists not to block innovation but to provide for the accountability and responsibility necessary for continuous improvement and involvement. All efforts should be focused on total cost solutions.

BEHAVIORAL STYLES

Behavioral styles and attitudes are changing in our world class environment. Management needs to create a positive climate that spreads throughout the organization. All levels of the organization need to promote "can do" programs which are results oriented and where people become assertive instead of aggressive. Let's look at some of the characteristics of aggressive and assertive behavior:

AGGRESSIVE

- Win at the expense of others' self-respect.
- Defeat any and all opposition.
- Protect one's turf with tooth and nail.
- Feel resentful when challenged or criticized.

ASSERTIVE

- Take a firm position without attacking others.
- Share feelings and facts to reduce misunderstandings.
- Invite trust and willingness to respond honestly.
- Recognize and respect rights of others.

It should be clear that the aggressive individual will have a difficult time working in a participative environment. The assertive person has the desired amount of group identification without losing the autonomy necessary for creative solutions.

DESIGNING AN ORGANIZATIONAL SURVEY

Part of the process of fostering both group identification and creative autonomy is taken up by people surveys which measure the strengths, weaknesses and needs of the organization's people. Besides identifying areas of opportunity for improving conditions, products or processes, surveys can also help to locate attitudinal problems and suggest ways to encourage people to take part in teams. Done correctly, as the following steps will show, a survey will eliminate fear and conjecture on the part of people who are not sure of what is coming. A survey will aid in revealing how people feel about their jobs, peers, supervisors and workplace. Collecting meaningful and accurate data is the result of careful planning and testing of a survey prior to its being given to an entire organization. We are now ready to look at the **Ten Steps for Designing a Survey**:

TEN STEPS
FOR DESIGNING A SURVEY

> **STEP ONE: Define Goals.** Describe the desired outcome of the survey. What kind of data will be obtained by this survey? In order to pinpoint what is to be accomplished by a survey, begin by establishing priorities. The checklist below will help you to prioritize needs:

Goals of an Organizational Survey

Number the following items from 1 to 10 in order of priority (10 being that item on which you would place the highest priority need).

_____ Define our organization's strengths and weaknesses.

_____ Evaluate our internal communication effectiveness.

_____ Realize how our people view their ability to work productively.

_____ Learn what motivates our people to achieve.

_____ Identify more effective ways of employing our resources.

_____ Become more responsive to our customer needs.

_____ Become more responsive to the needs of our people.

_____ Encourage our people to contribute ideas for improvement.

_____ Develop leadership skills at all levels.

_____ Improve our organization's ability to perform.

STEP TWO: Target the Group. Who is the group from which the data will be gathered? Will it be one segment of the organization such as those directly involved with production, or will the target group be everyone in the organization? The answer to this question is determined by the goals that you have defined above. What group or groups can provide you with the information that will help you achieve that goal? Don't limit yourself, however, to traditional areas when looking at the achievement of goals. For example, if your goal is to better relations with your customers, surveying your Sales and Customer Service departments is an obvious place to start. But what about Design Engineering? They may have an idea for improving design that nobody has listened to. Or Purchasing may know of some superior materials which reduce production time and improve quality. The Quality department can also provide a great deal of insight into technical and quantitative information from customers. The best solutions come from the interaction of many diverse elements in a team setting.

STEP THREE: Determine the Survey Sample. It is often unrealistic to survey everyone in the target group because it contains too many members. The solution is to take a representative portion of the target group and extrapolate conclusions from the results of the survey sample. Selecting this sample rests on two principles:

1. The sample must be representative. It shouldn't consist of only one gender or just supervisors, but should accurately reflect all the diverse sectors within the target group's population.

2. The sample must be randomly selected. That means that all members of the target group have an equal chance of being selected for inclusion in the sample.

STEP FOUR: Develop the Questionnaire. A comprehensive survey asks people to respond to statements which address the following areas:

- Current job activities.
- Relationship with supervisors and peers.
- Structure of the organization.
- Organization's ability to perform effectively.

Whether your survey covers all these areas or some subset, the package you present to the people in your company must contain four parts. They are:

• A cover letter — Should clearly state the purpose of the survey, how results will be used and when they will be shared as well as guarantee the anonymity of the respondent.

• The items (questions or statements) — Should also be clear and to the point. Make sure each item asks only one question or addresses only one issue so that there is no ambiguity. Word them so that any bias is removed. Don't use language that could be interpreted as a threat to the people taking the survey. For example:

	AGREE					DISAGREE	
1	2	3	4	5	6	7	8

Salespeople who don't meet their quotas should be laid off first in a slowdown.

Such a statement will look like you already have a plan to do just what the sentence says.

• The scales — Should range from strong positive feelings to strong negative feelings. Some of the more popular scales are below:

1. To a very great extent — To a very little extent.
2. Strongly agree — Strongly disagree.
3. Always — Never.

• The codes — Should indicate how to handle problem responses or no response to an item. It should also indicate the score, or point value, of each item. This section obviously is for the people who will compile the results.

STEP FIVE: Pretest the Questionnaire. In order to fine tune the questionnaire, pretest a small group from those people who will be surveyed. Examine the results to determine whether the responses are skewed or whether they are balanced on either side of the issue. Equally important is to interview the pretest group after the survey to see whether they understood the items or not. In both cases, adjust the items to elicit a more specific response and to make them more clear.

STEP SIX: Prepare the Final Draft. Correct any problems identified in the previous step and prepare an easy-to-read final draft.

STEP SEVEN: Administer the Questionnaire. Distribute the cover letter and questionnaire to all that will participate within the targeted group. Define a time frame for completion of the survey and give precise directions for turning it in. Consider a special mailing to people's homes or a payroll check stuffer.

STEP EIGHT: Code the Responses. Create a coding system that identifies the origin of the responses. Factors to consider coding include: department, sex, position in organization, age and any other factor which might add value to the survey results or identify bias in the design of the survey. Here is a sample:

DEPARTMENT (if multiple, list)
    Circle one:
    123   456   789   101   112   131

SEX
    Circle one:
    M   F

POSITION
    Circle one:
    Assembler
    Supervisor
    Manager

STEP NINE: Tabulate the Results. Transfer the information from each completed survey to a master which compiles the results of all the surveys. The outcome will reveal how many individuals responded to each question and how many responded to each degree in the selected scale.

ALWAYS									NEVER
1	2	3	4	5	6	7	8	9	10

STEP TEN: Prepare the Report. Analyze the results of the survey tabulation. Are any trends revealed? Does there seem to be a common attitude that exists among those surveyed? Does the survey point out specific areas of opportunity where improvements can be effected? The report should include the statistical results of the survey as well as comments related to an analysis of the results. Some reports also include written comments by the participants if these are asked for.

SURVEYS AND FEEDBACK

All well-designed organizational surveys have an eleventh step: Give prompt feedback to the participants in the survey. Feedback shows that you are serious about the survey and, more importantly, that you are serious about people involvement/empowerment. Results of the survey can be distributed through short memos, reports, newsletters, voluntary discussion sessions and even bulletin boards. Survey results can also work to bring groups together for the first time as they talk about what the results mean and what should be done. In a certain sense, feedback is the means for gaining grassroots activism. The purpose of surveys and feedback is to get people talking to each other so they will be motivated to change what needs improvement.

MOTIVATION

Motivating people is vital to the success of any improvement activity. The most important thing a company can do is seek people involvement/empowerment from the outset. This is an essential part of any motivational effort. You need to be sure as well that people understand the relationship between the rewards of participation and improving company functions. A company's best chance of motivating people is to understand their personal needs and integrate them with the needs of the company. Therefore, we believe that the best encouragement management can offer is the promotion of a people involvement and empowerment process in which there are opportunities to participate in the implementation of their own ideas.

In our extensive consultations, we have noted three basic ways to motivate people:

1. **Fear — "If you don't do this, I'll fire you!"**

2. **Bribery — "If you do this, I'll give you a raise."**

3. **Internally motivate them by understanding the application of Maslow's hierarchy of needs.**

Threats and bribes are very powerful, but short lived. People involvement/empowerment, however, satisfies the highest of the needs that psychologist Abraham Maslow hypothesized — self-fulfillment. Let's take a brief look at Maslow's hierarchy of needs and how they apply to people involvement/empowerment.

Physiological needs — At this level, people work in order to pay their bills and take care of themselves and their families.

Security needs — Here, people want to know that their job is secure and that they work in an environment which is orderly and comfortable.

Social needs — People at this level of need are looking to be part of a team effort. They want to work for a company that treats its employees as a valuable partner.

Self-esteem needs — At this level of the hierarchy, people are looking for recognition for their accomplishments and for the respect of their fellow workers and of management.

Self-fulfillment needs — At the pinnacle of needs, people are looking to develop to their full potential. They want to explore new areas, learn new skills and find out what they are capable of accomplishing as an individual.

Any company which plans to embark upon a people involvement/ empowerment process better be aware of these needs. It is foolish to start such a process and expect success if people are upset about wages and unsafe working conditions.

If these more basic needs are not being met, then you would have to start an involvement/empowerment process at a much lower level. People would need to talk about how to improve working conditions and they would have to believe that management was serious about changing them if the process was to be successful. In short, any motivational effort must take the entire hierarchy of needs into account.

After all, you don't start training to run a marathon by running 26 miles on the first day. First of all, you need to know the physical condition of your body and then you need to advance slowly through a regimen of increasing difficulty. The same principle applies to a people involvement and empowerment process.

PRINCIPLES OF PARTICIPATION

All that we have discussed in this chapter can be summarized in a few principles of participation. Many psychologists believe as we do that a more meaningful work experience in which people are fulfilling all of their personal needs is the single best motivator and, as such, works toward making the company the best it can be.

People involvement/empowerment is defined as a process in which people participate in continuous improvement. As you can see, the psychological and manufacturing processes mirror each other. Both aim to make people feel part of a team. The foundation of this process is a philosophy which encompasses the three principles found in the following chart.

THE PRINCIPLES OF PARTICIPATION

- **People desire a meaningful work experience.**

- **An individual has unique knowledge about the job he or she performs.**

- **People are a valuable resource for productivity improvement.**

These principles are the thinking upon which people involvement/ empowerment is based. Companies must adopt this philosophy before participation will become productive. Let's look more closely at what we mean by each principle.

Meaningful work experience — People will become increasingly interested in their work if they are allowed to make contributions which affect the results of their work and if they have opportunities to participate in decision making. Employees in the past have been treated more like workhorses. A workhorse was trained to stand in front of the plow and pull as the farmer tilled the field. The horse was not self-motivated. It did its work at the prodding of the farmer. Traditional employee and employer relationships are not much different. The worker is motivated only by a paycheck at the end of the week. Every day, he does his job because he must.

Self-motivation, on the other hand, occurs when an individual sets out to make a difference. People seek out experiences which are fulfilling, that is, experiences in which they feel that their contribution has made a difference. And work has increasingly become one of the places where fulfillment exists for many people.

Unique knowledge — The second principle of participation acknowledges the unique expertise of the individual worker. In the past, we thought that the way to solve a factory floor problem was behind the closed door of a conference room. Information about the problem was supposedly obtained from workers and offered by supervisors and engineers as data in a problem solving session. The unique knowledge of the people directly involved in the problem remained on the factory floor.

This is like having the maître d' tell the chef how to cook dinner. People on the job are resident experts. They make things happen under the existing work conditions. They can directly provide pertinent data about a problem and offer possible solutions. In fact, if given authority and responsibility, they can solve the problem by themselves. Why muddy up the water by passing ideas back and forth through several layers of bureaucracy? The people on the field doing the work have a perspective that those on the sidelines don't have. The players know how the proposed solutions will fit into current work patterns. They are, after all, the people who would be affected by the chosen solution.

Valuable productivity resource — This principle requires having faith in the power of people who work within an organization that they can add something of value to a product or service provided by the business. In many instances, the solution to a problem may not be obvious until the issues and concerns surrounding the problem have been openly discussed. That is when the good ideas start to surface. The participatory organization must be devoted to discovering the source of these ideas and allowing them to surface. While working at Allied Signal, for example, we remember loving to go to the floor in order to get the real "scoop" from the people we stopped and talked to. We had a better idea of what was going on after getting their thoughts.

PARTICIPATION AND THE CHANGE PROCESS

The implementation of a process of people involvement and empowerment will be a big change for any company. There are many factors to consider and a small change in one area can have large and unforeseen consequences in another area. Leaders of this change process must be aware of individual psychological needs, social patterns, company operations and processes, industry activities, national economics and the global marketplace. The next chapter looks at the characteristics of change and explores how companies can institute a change process with the least amount of disruption to the people whose work is affected by the changes and to the company itself.

Chapter Three

INSTITUTING
THE
CHANGE
PROCESS

INSTITUTING
THE
CHANGE
PROCESS

Business is like New England weather. Whatever the conditions are now, chances are they will be different in a short while. Snow, bitter winds today; sunny, mild tomorrow. It's got to the point where native New Englanders don't even think such sudden shifts are unusual. Change is expected.

The business which recognizes change as a given is already far ahead of the game. Such a company is in a position to control the effects of change in ways that are most beneficial to the organization. This company might fly a banner, like the one depicted here, above its front door:

The "Δ" symbol is the Greek letter delta which is used in mathematics and science to represent change. The circle which surrounds "Δ" represents control, or an attempt to confine change within specified boundaries. The rest of this chapter will show you just how to encircle "Δ," or change, in order to become its master rather than letting change master you. An astute company encourages change but provides clear guidelines within which change can take place.

In a certain sense, managing change is the same as integrating left and right brain functions. The left brain is analytical. Its counterparts in business are reporting and control systems, quantitative measures and budgets. The right brain is holistic. Its counterparts are the company vision, strategic hunches and the "big picture." The left brain focuses on and measures what the company has done and is doing. The right brain looks ahead to what the company can be. Both attributes are necessary for change. Measuring where a company is and has been gives us a sense of corporate history. We don't want to repeat the same mistakes while instituting a change process. Envisioning where a company is headed will give us a reason to change.

RESISTANCE TO CHANGE

As companies move toward world class status, there will be some resistance to the push for change in the organization. Overcoming this resistance is a challenge that is best met by educating people about the opportunities that change represents. One of the benefits which should be stressed is the pride and sense of accomplishment which comes from helping to build and then work in a world class company. Beyond these morale boosters, however, a company should be prepared not only to have everyone participate in the challenges, but to share in the benefits.

When we have been called in to assess resistance at a company, we have discovered that most problems usually are the result of one of these conditions:

- Teams believe that management is out looking for a scapegoat, somebody or some group to blame for everything that is going wrong.

- People believe that the change process is just a way for management to check up on their performance so that people can be laid off.

- People know what the problems are and who is causing them, but they can't say because of loyalty to a fellow worker or fear of a supervisor or management.

- People have worked in a crisis management environment where change has come to represent out of control conditions. The resultant negative stress leads to behavior in which people avoid the source of change.

- Teams are a waste of time. Management never listens to them. Besides, we tried this ten years ago and nothing changed ...

Our strong advice is not to allow these attitudes and feelings to remain suppressed. Bring them out in the open and discuss them fully and honestly. Only in this way can you start to build the sense of trust between people and management which is so essential to the people involvement/empowerment process. One method we have used is to list the above conditions and ask team members whether any or all are in effect at your company. Open discussion of these issues in a team setting is the most effective method of overcoming resistance to change. It is rare to have change successfully imposed from the upper levels of an organization. Change is easiest and most successful as a grassroots process.

Understanding how people handle change is important. Studies on how people deal with the death of a loved one show that there are five stages that one must go through in order to deal with the death. Psychologists theorize that people go through similar, if not the same, stages when dealing with change in the workplace. The acronym "SARAH" is a memory aid for these five stages.

```
S = SHOCK
A = ANGER
R = REJECTION
A = ACKNOWLEDGMENT
H = HOPE or HELP
```

Management needs to recognize these phases and encourage people to transition through them in order to become truly empowered.

STRATEGY FOR CHANGE

Strategy is a plan of action which has been formulated to achieve an end. As with most plans of action, the strategy for implementing a people involvement/empowerment process begins by realizing and defining the need for change. Once the need is established, then you can begin determining and reviewing competitive issues. Management should not suppress any of the issues which surround the effects of change. Being competitive in a world class marketplace means achieving a level of excellence in which strategy shapes and is, in turn, shaped by your corporate culture. You want to create a culture in which desirable traits are developed with careful attention to the needs of the organization as well as the needs of the people. Culture and strategy unite in a common purpose.

The strategy for change reminds us of what one woman who reached her 105th birthday had to say. She attributed her longevity to her "gracious acceptance of change."

The next part of your strategy is to conduct a survey to obtain more information about the need for improvement and to disseminate this information throughout the organization. You can then identify specific areas as a starting point for a team. The process of people involvement/empowerment should never start unless these real needs or opportunities are identified. Such areas often fall into two categories: 1) cost savings, and 2) people development. People development, of course, helps teams and their companies realize the first area of opportunity.

When opportunities have been identified, a team should concentrate on forming objectives and goals which will serve to direct the team's emphasis. Some items to consider which have an impact on the organization are time schedules, equipment and tooling needs and human resources. Measurements should be put into place early in the program to help teams meet goals. These measurements, of course, should be developed by the team and not imposed upon them from higher levels of the organization.

THE BASICS OF FOSTERING CHANGE

A company needs to pay attention to four basic areas in order to assist in the change process. They are the following:

> - **Motivation.**
> - **Role modeling.**
> - **Training.**
> - **Performance measurement.**

Motivation. Motivation operates on two levels — the company and personal level. At the company level, we are motivated to change by competition, cost reduction, new products and the global marketplace. On the personal level, people are motivated by recognition, pay increases, promotions or the fear of being out of a job. Whatever the motivator, it is important to turn it into an area of opportunity. Remember what the philosopher, Plato, said: People change for one of two reasons — fear or hope.

Role modeling. Role modeling also operates on two levels. On the first level, a company needs to find leaders in the employee involvement/empowerment process. These companies can provide you with the necessary justification and guidelines to begin the process yourself. This introduces the second level in which one person becomes the champion and acts as a personal role model. There can be champions that act company-wide and champions that act within the sphere of a team.

Training. Although we have repeatedly mentioned training as a key to a successful people involvement/empowerment process, it bears repeating again. The skills needed to work together as a team to solve problems and develop opportunities are the most important components of any program. Training often breaks down into two areas as well. They are training in team building and dynamics and training in specific areas such as Statistical Process Control, set-up reduction or problem solving. The aim of training is to help people internalize behaviors which will be helpful to them and the company.

Performance measurement. Performance measurements are critical to the continuous improvement process. Not only do they tell people where they are, but where they have come from. Thus, they act as both a motivator and a feedback mechanism which will spur on even greater improvement. Just because measurement is listed last, that does not mean it is the last thing to do or the least important. Performance measurement has a quantitative and qualitative effect.

GUIDELINES FOR THE BEHAVIORAL PROCESS

As you probably have already noted, implementing a strategy for change rests largely on providing teams with information and necessary resources, not with imposing control and structure from above. In our work, we have noted several guidelines which have proven essential for this process to be most successful.

First, excellence will be maximized when a company's culture and strategy work together harmoniously. Earlier, we mentioned desirable traits to develop in a company culture. We have found the following to be absolutely necessary:

- **Commitment to purpose.**
- **Delivery of commitment through performance.**
- **Dedication to commitment.**

Commitment to purpose. This means that all the people in a company understand and accept the goals of the organization. Top management commitment is displayed through their day-to-day behavior. The organizational goals must be made visible through on-going communication between all levels of a business organization.

Delivery of commitment through performance. With the added insight on business goals, people will be prepared to do what it takes to deliver on the commitment via continuously improving performance.

Dedication to commitment. Thinking and actions must be dedicated to the organization's purpose. The people need to work in a united effort. A company mission statement is one way to provide this direction. Often, however, they are developed only to "keep up with the Joneses." The test we propose for any company mission statement is this:

> **Is the day-to-day behavior
> of management
> and non-management
> consistent
> with the company mission statement?**

Second on our list of necessary guidelines is the need to nurture and encourage creativity at all levels of an organization. Creativity, or innovation, is a critical tool in maintaining a competitive edge and in ensuring long-term business vitality. If there is one reason for the Far East's success, it must be this unlocking of creativity. For them, it was necessary. They lacked the raw materials and natural resources that we have so they had to think of ways to build products more efficiently. Their organizations encourage innovation; ours, all too often, work to stifle it.

Rosabeth Moss Kanter, in the film "The Change Masters," identifies several ways in which innovation is stifled. If we want to continue to run our companies improperly, she "advises" us to be suspicious of any creative solutions which originate in the lower levels of an organization. If you are going to set up a suggestion system, she continues, make sure that any idea which may get implemented has to go through several layers of approval before actual work can be done. Be free with criticism and stingy with praise. Control every facet of the organization and make sure that nobody knows how or what you are controlling. And never forget, Kanter says, that those on top already know everything there is to know about running the business.

You may be laughing at this disastrous manner of running a company, but we see this type of thinking all the time. We also see companies which encourage innovation or which have adopted our process for encouraging innovation. Here is what we recommend:

- Remove all departmental walls and other obstructions which block the free exchange of information.

- Let teams act within guidelines which forego the need for layers of approval before action can be taken.

- Provide people with all the education, training and resources necessary to do it right the first time.

- Be open to all new ideas and praise all efforts to seek continuous improvement.

- Believe in the process and the results will follow.

Third on our list of behavioral guidelines is a three-part approach to educating people about the people involvement/empowerment process.

The first step is **Instruction (Learning Theory).** In a formalized training session, the rationale for people involvement/empowerment must be explained along with how it works and what is to be gained.

The second step is **Citing Examples.** In this approach, examples of how this process has been successful in other organizations are highlighted. If a company has done benchmarking as part of its Total Quality Management (TQM) process, utilize that information. Case histories focus on why there was a need to change and how the process was able to affect productivity improvement. Whenever possible, instructors for this step should come from the organizations which are cited. This way, the instructor can respond first hand to any questions which may come up in discussions.

The third step is **Simulation.** People learn in this step about the process by participating in the solution of hypothetical problems. An educational program that integrates theory with practice through simulation will give people a broad educational experience upon which future progress can be built. This three-step approach is reinforced by a philosophy which Confucius stated many, many years ago.

**"What I hear, I forget.
What I see, I remember.
What I do, I understand."**

We think those words are a fitting summation of the guidelines for the behavioral process of change.

HOW TO COPE WITH PROBLEM PERSONNEL

We all know that any endeavor which includes human beings is not perfect. There will be some people or groups of people who are more reticent than others and who lack trust or who have been hurt by company policy changes in the past. Your job is to go more than halfway in solving these problems. One bad apple *can* spoil the whole bushel. Your company will need to recognize people needs and balance them with the needs of the organization.

Management must work in cooperation with the people in an organization on a variety of tasks. Coping with people's distrust and fears needs to be addressed through visible organizational structures and job descriptions which promote the expected participatory level. Management must turn negative motivation factors into positive ones which generate pride. All people have the same basic needs. They want to be involved in constructive teams that work together with management in improving the company and creating a better place to work. Paying attention to that need will do more to solve personnel problems than any other technique.

In our work at Loran, a small manufacturer of audio cassettes, we came across an excellent example of why teamwork must be a two-way street between management and the people. Before we came to assist at their plant, the people were formed into what they believed to be teams. One of the problems they were working on was with a mold in which only 4 of the sixteen cavities were working. The team decided it needed a new mold and told management. Management asked how much it would cost. The team said it didn't know but that it would find out.

Some time went by and the team determined the cost of making the new mold in-house. The price, which they presented to management, was in the thousands of dollars. Management then wanted to know what the benefits were if they invested this much money in a new mold. The project then died at this point.

A year later when we came on the scene, the team told us that management had just sat on their suggestion. The team felt that management really didn't care about having them participate.

We told the team to look at what happened from management's side for a moment. You gave them a price and no alternative solutions. You didn't tell them how fast they would get their investment back. The team saw what we were pointing out and we worked together to come up with competitive costs for having the mold made outside and with cost justifications and paybacks.

With that information in hand and a projected payback of six months, management became heavily involved in finding a way to get a new mold. Management even involved the team in evaluating a mold manufacturer in Portugal, which the team determined was a more cost-effective and higher quality producer than Loran at making the mold. The lesson to be learned is that there really wasn't a personnel problem here, but a team which was not properly trained and facilitated in cost justification and analysis.

As for specific problems, here are some suggestions we have used and found to be helpful in demonstrating motivation.

The manager or supervisor is the problem. This happens more than we care to admit. It is difficult for a person who is used to having complete power to share control with others. We have three solutions:

- Use a survey to gather facts about leadership and share the results with the person.

- Use an outside observer who will fairly judge the manager or supervisor.

- Send the manager or supervisor to some team building and leadership seminars, workshops or training sessions.

There is a conflict between people. Whenever possible, the people should solve this problem between themselves. If this isn't possible, then an impartial facilitator can be used to iron out any differences. Another suggestion is to have the team leader address the issue in the confines of the team and let the team members help with a solution. This can be done in the following steps:

1. Go one-on-one with each affected person and get their side of the story.
2. Gather facts about the conflict.
3. Ascertain what happened, when and to whom.
4. Get together with all the affected people.
5. Facilitate a discussion to resolve the problem and provide direction as needed.

There is one person who always creates roadblocks. The best way to handle this problem is to educate the individual again about the benefits to be gained through people involvement/empowerment. Often, this won't be necessary because the team will confront the individual causing the problem and emphasize benefits. Another technique which has always worked is to allow the problem individual to meet privately with the team leader. The individual is given an hour to present his or her side, but must then listen to the team leader's side. We have seen the most argumentative people come out of such meetings and emerge as the team's most outspoken advocates. Sometimes, people just need some attention and a chance to vent their displeasure or they need to hear reassurance that their participation means something.

GAINING SUPPORT AND "BUY-IN"

For any people involvement/empowerment process to be successful, it will need the full support of the people who are participating. Above all, people must understand that this process is a continuous striving for improvement and not just a one-time event. Equally as important is the necessity of allowing people to "buy in" to the process and not to force them into it. JAL, Japan Airlines, accomplishes this with a concept called *kizuki* which are elite corps of engineers who are assigned to their own 747s. They then become obsessed with performance. When a team "owns" what it is doing, the level of excellence increases dramatically.

Management can also help the process of "buying in" by demonstrating it themselves. Recently a company initiated a people involvement/empowerment process and, to show their commitment, management took pay cuts up to 15 percent. Management can also obtain support by informing its people about the market and competition the company is up against. The key here is to treat people as important components who have the need to know how to do their job better. Let people know why it is important to reduce costs, to modernize, to change from the old ways of doing business to the new ways. The best way to institute the change process is to show that you believe in it.

Part of the new way of doing business is structuring the work force into a unified whole. No change process is complete without a vision of what employee involvement/empowerment means. The next chapter introduces this critical area.

Chapter Four

STRUCTURING
THE
WORK
FORCE

STRUCTURING
THE
WORK
FORCE

Everybody is talking about the need for a company to have a vision of what it is and where it wants to be. The concept is painted as a sort of Camelot where there is peace and plenty for everybody and all we have to do is dream about it and it will come true. Much of the talk about the establishment of a company vision discusses an amorphous Eden on the horizon. All too often that Eden is a mirage, instead of the hoped-for oasis.

With the implementation of a people involvement/empowerment program, however, the vision on the horizon which your company wants to achieve can be a place where there is prosperity. It will not be heaven, but it will be a real accomplishment and not a false hope. For instance, it has been reported that companies which have adopted an employee stock ownership plan (ESOP) and which allow their people to actively engage in guiding the company, experience growth rates of 8 to 11% faster than companies which stifle people participation. As always, people involvement/ empowerment makes good business sense.

It does at Specialized Bicycle Components, a $74 million dollar California company, which encourages people to indulge in their love of biking. Two-hour rides at lunchtime are not uncommon. The result is that everybody in the company, including service and sales representatives, are well-versed in the art, science and mechanics of biking. This pays off many times over when dealers or customers have questions. Specialized's involved and empowered people have the answers.

Even large companies, such as Traveler's Insurance, have found that involving their people in an ongoing training program which empowers them to rise through the ranks decreases the turnover rate. In an article in the **Connecticut Business Industry Association News**, Robert S. Fenn, national director of training, points out that another benefit is work of higher quality.

MANAGEMENT OF THE FUTURE: An Attitudinal Change

Companies, large and small, are discovering that the 1990s present another challenge in terms of involving people. The American work force will be an ethnically, racially and culturally diverse group of people which will include both sexes at all levels. It is not enough, of course, just to recognize this fact. Real change begins with evaluating your own attitudes toward different groups of people. People involvement/empowerment programs are designed so that people and managers do learn to accept differences and still work together for the common good. This is because the team concept believes that all people have something of value to contribute.

In an interview that James A. Autry, president of the Meredith Corporation's magazine division, recently gave to *Executive Strategies* about his new book, **Love and Profit** (Morrow), he stated that the attitudinal change necessary for the 1990s is not wimpy. Caring is a great way to boost productivity from your staff. What Autry identifies as the "drill-sergeant approach" is no longer effective. People can no longer be intimidated into increasing productivity. Autry says that the best way to improve your profit picture is to earn the respect of the people you manage by first respecting them.

CREATING A VISION

What are the common ingredients of those companies which have been able to implement successful people involvement/empowerment programs? From our experience in the field, we have been able to isolate five factors:

1 **The commitment of top management.** This is where the formulation of a vision must start. That vision must be driven by the marketplace in concert with the strategic plan. It helps to answer the question: "What do we want to be when we grow up?" The vision must not be one handed down from on high. It should be more like the Ten Commandments, rules whereby people can take responsibility and be granted the authority to create a better company.

2 **Total participation of management.** How does the old saying go? What's good for the goose is good for the gander. Never, never, expect people to engage in a process of which you aren't willing to take part. Management must realize that they are a service organiza-

tion for the employees. They are management's internal customer and, as such, management must be in constant communication with them. That is, management must act as a supplier to the people.

3 **Participation by people.** The old days of "us" and "them" are over. The people who work at a company are every bit as important as management. They should be listened to. Listening is one of the steps used in gaining participation.

4 **Involvement of the individual.** Although we all have a basic need to belong and work in groups, we have an equally strong desire to get individual enjoyment. Every people involvement/empowerment program must contain an element of personal satisfaction.

5 **Continuous improvement teams.** This is the grassroots action level of people involvement/empowerment programs. Without teams, the process will become a management only program. As we have found out in the past, such programs are never as effective as ones that are activated by people.

One effective way to help people become aware of a company's vision is to allow them to participate in the development of statements which convey the mission of both the company and its people. The involvement in the development of the vision acts as a motivator in making quality the primary responsibility of all people. Quality as a way of life should be in all company vision statements.

One of the best definitions of quality we have ever read was made by Rod Canion, Compaq's founder, former CEO and president, in an issue of the *Harvard Business Review*. He said that "quality isn't whether or not your products work. Quality is how people do their jobs. Quality is defining your job and then meeting expectations." We would certainly encourage everybody to put something like that in their company's statement.

Kinder Care Learning Centers also found that giving their people a vision helped pull the company together. The message that management gave was that Kinder Care was a company of people who were providing care to other people (children) so that their parents (also people!) could feel safe as they went off to work and provide for their families. Kinder Care was able to motivate their own people by creating a vision in which the company was more than another day care center. They were a group of people who could and would make a difference in the lives of children.

PEOPLE INVOLVEMENT/EMPOWERMENT

The mission of every company is to involve and to empower people to solve problems and find areas of opportunity. One method to do this is to use the old-fashioned idea box with a new twist. Researchers have found that the Japanese way of soliciting many small solutions is far more effective than our insistence on finding and rewarding only the big solutions. Since in their process everybody is rewarded to some extent, far more people participate which, in turn, generates a feeling of involvement and empowerment. Management should also seek out dissent, rather than stamping out opposition. The good leader knows that dissent points out things that must be addressed. Never give a cold shoulder to people who disagree with you.

In order to achieve a successful people involvement/empowerment program, we have developed ten steps to follow:

---

10 STEPS TO SUCCESSFUL
PEOPLE INVOLVEMENT/EMPOWERMENT

1 **Obtain information on attitudes and morale.**

2 **Understand how behavior affects the company and how resistance manifests.**

3 **Evaluate these attitudes and behaviors.**

4 **Establish an open door policy and an open mind concept.**

5 **Become an effective listener.**

6 **Use time effectively to avoid the common pitfall of not enough time to do, listen, collect data, learn.**

7 **Provide tools — education/training in latest techniques, technologies, etc.**

8 **Measure results of team activities to show interest.**

9 **Reward people/teams for performance stages.**

10 **Don't procrastinate; make decisions.**

The list on the previous page sums up what has been covered so far on how to implement a people involvement/empowerment program. Now let's look at some specific techniques to use and some specific situations you may encounter.

JOB #1: TRAINING THE TEAM

Most companies underestimate the amount of training needed to enable people involvement/empowerment programs to succeed, according to a survey conducted by the Association for Quality and Participation, Development Dimensions International and *Industry Week*. The survey, in fact, found that 54 percent of the managers said training was inadequate. This was their conclusion even though most companies do provide some training in the areas of problem solving, communication skills, new job skills and interpersonal dynamics. What makes the task of training difficult is that people involvement/empowerment programs require people to be generalists, not specialists. That means everybody needs training in all the areas mentioned above.

Barr Labs has a very appropriate way to describe incomplete or inadequate training. They call such one-shot programs an "Education Injection." It is decidedly not what they do at their company. At Barr Labs, training and education are part of a continuous improvement cycle. For instance, the human resources department keeps a record of all new employees. When that number reaches roughly 30 to 40 people, they begin an education session in which they are given instruction in Total Quality Management (TQM). This session lasts for a minimum of two hours and often extends to six hours of instruction. This session is in addition to orientations which instruct new employees in the philosophies of people involvement/empowerment.

Company officials at Barr Labs report that people value the instructional sessions. The company has also found that their program has the added benefit of working to help people who change jobs or get promoted. The men and women at Barr Labs feel that the company is communicating with them, that people are being "grown" in the sense that they are allowed to pursue avenues which will benefit them and the company.

MOTIVATION

The leader of the company of the future will also need to train himself or herself to be more of a facilitator and coach who empowers people than a drill sergeant. Your power to lead is directly proportional to the trust people place in you because they think you will do a good job. Sometimes this trust can come from making people laugh and feel good. Sometimes it can be strengthened by other activities.

Ben and Jerry's, the famous ice cream maker, has a Joy Committee whose only function is to think of ways to relieve the stress of working. Anybody who has visited their plant in Vermont is immediately aware of the company's sense of humor. The Joy Gang, as it has come to be known, has a $10,000 budget and the obvious support of co-founder Jerry Greenfield who attends two-thirds of the meetings, but who does not run them. Some of the ideas that the Joy Gang has come up with: Ping-pong tournaments, Cajun extravaganzas, Tacky Dress-up Days and a group novel. You don't have to be as wild as Ben and Jerry, but company trips to amusement parks, semi-annual dinners, birthday presents are also effective. Here at Pro-Tech, for example, we combine our company meetings with a couple of days of fun and sun at the hotel, dinners at top-notch local restaurants here in Florida as well as a plain fun activity like an afternoon cruise on a yacht.

Motivation, oddly enough to some of you, can also be increased by allowing and even encouraging dissent. Many experts, including us, believe that management should solicit disagreement at team meetings. Dissent serves several functions:

- It prevents the person who makes a decision from believing that his or her ideas are the only good ones.

- It places other ideas on the docket, alternatives that may eventually prove to be better.

- It acts as a catalyst to encourage more ideas and alternatives.

Encouraging dissent makes people trust you more, if you are sincerely willing to listen to what you or the company may be doing wrong. Just make sure that everybody understands this one rule:

**Disagree with the idea, not the person
and suggest an alternative
whenever possible.**

IDEA SYSTEMS

Another way to involve people is to implement an idea system for alternatives and other ideas. The Japanese suggestion box, which rewards all people who participate, is a far better motivator than the American system which rewards a few people with larger sums of money. The American system ignores the fact that most progress is made in small increments, not in big breakthroughs. The Japanese system also makes people feel as though they are more involved. In addition, it is easier to implement and run because the system itself is cost-effective and simple.

Above all, an idea system should put people in the mind-set of continuous improvement. If people are taught to do simple cost/benefit analyses and include them with the idea, you will find that not only does the company cut costs, but it gains a more competent work force who are looking for even more areas of opportunity.

It should be noted that traditional suggestion systems represent a low level of employee involvement/empowerment. This is due to the fact that suggestions are made and then passed up to management for judgment. We believe this system, which will work in the interim, will eventually be an adjunct to team-based problem solving.

TECHNIQUES IN A UNION ENVIRONMENT

The basic rule in union environments is to include union personnel from the very beginning in the implementation of a people involvement/empowerment program. To many members of management, unions are seen as roadblocks. This was the attitude in the auto industry until Japan proved that you can expect and get high quality from union people if you give them an opportunity to be involved.

NUMMI (New United Motor Manufacturing, Inc.), for example, made an agreement with the United Auto Workers (UAW) before it began sending out employment applications. The agreement and the applications spelled out that quality would be the responsibility of everybody who worked at NUMMI. One indication of the effectiveness of people involvement/empowerment is the rate of absenteeism at the old Freemont facility and the new NUMMI facility. At the old company, absenteeism often reached 25 percent. At NUMMI, it averages 4 to 5 percent.

It should be noted here that the legality of people involvement/ empowerment programs has been brought into question by the National Labor Relations Board. Some groups have protested that these programs inhibit people's ability to form labor groups independent of the company. The *Wall Street Journal* points out that "the stakes are enormous." According to estimates put out by the Labor Department, people participation programs are used by approximately one-third of the larger companies in this country.

While consulting at J.I. Case, a strong United Auto Workers plant, we were witness to some initial negative reactions from union leadership. This feeling soon disappeared, however, when company management decided to share the power and gave full management of the company's Employee Involvement (EI) program to union personnel. The union established teams and then determined what types of education and training they wanted us at Pro-Tech to provide. Not only were the people happy to be treated like individuals, but the savings generated from the EI program eventually made it self-funding.

If you think union people won't buy in to people involvement/ empowerment, you're wrong. Here's another example from a client that we are always happy to talk about.

People involvement/empowerment does not upset Judy Contreras, the union representative on the Pegasus team at the Northvale, NJ, plant of Barr Labs, a producer of generic drugs. On the contrary, she's been waiting for years for management to use this approach. Not until a shake-up two years ago did she think it was possible and even then she wasn't sure. She remembers being afraid to approach Gerry Price, the new executive vice president.

Three years before, Contreras had read up on employee involvement as part of her work on a negotiating committee for her union, the Oil, Chemical, Atomic Workers (OCAW) #8-149. In fact, she helped write up a labor/management participation program. She summoned up the courage to hand it over to Price to read and was floored when he said that it was a great plan. She later found out that Price had already worked on similar programs with us in his position as vice president-manufacturing at L'Oréal Corporation, the cosmetics manufacturer. Price then sent a group of people, including Contreras and Chris Samulowitz, then corporate director of human resources, to the Dover, DE, plant of General Foods where we were helping the people there adopt World Class/JIT principles.

Contreras still remembers how surprised and pleased she was. "I saw that what I had been reading about while preparing the labor/management participation program could really happen."

When she came back to Barr Labs, she spoke to the union stewards who were at first against any changes, but she finally convinced them to give employee involvement a chance.

"The company listened to our input and feelings," Contreras says of the company. "They trusted that the people who have been working here for years could solve the problems."

Contreras also points out that the company worked with local schools in setting up classes for remedial reading and math. To

Samulowitz, these are the subtleties that make the difference between success and failure. He notes that Barr Labs also began employee assistance programs, day care and professional training as well as hiring a trained counselor.

"We want to fully integrate the experience of working here with all their life," says Samulowitz. "Even in the home and community, we want to show these people that we're here to help."

MANAGING FEAR OF THE UNKNOWN

The very simple solution to this problem is to make those who are afraid, knowledgeable and confident. This robs fear of its powerful hold over people. People resist change, as we have already noted, because it upsets the normal way of doing things. The fear of an unknown process, even one in which people are involved and empowered, creates a sense of discomfort and anxiety in people. Management needs to counter these feelings with a different set of values which are more participative in nature. Being involved and empowered gives people a good feeling about themselves and that translates into a good feeling about the change process because it allows them to be a force in making their future happen.

INFORMAL ORGANIZATIONS

One way to understand the fear of change is to become familiar with how your organization lines up along informal lines. Informal organizations, the network of social and personal interactions among people, often reveal valuable information. To study informal organizations, you first of all have to know their characteristics. Such groups are usually small and personal and they exist at all levels of the company. Leadership, which is also informally granted, is earned and given by group members. Informal organizations exist parallel to formal company hierarchies. Various sociologists and organizational psychologists have recognized that informal organizations have four functions:

> • **Maintain company values.**
> • **Satisfy social needs.**
> • **Ease communication.**
> • **Keep social control.**

Now perhaps you can see why it is so important to see how you can blend these informal functions with the needs of the formal organization.

In order to study informal organizations, we suggest taking the following steps:

> 1 **Observe people and relationships, not what they are producing or servicing.**
>
> 2 **Watch how they interact with each other.**
>
> 3 **Keep a record of the ways they reach an agreement.**
>
> 4 **Find out what principles and ideas they agree and disagree about.**

INTEGRATION OF TECHNOLOGY

One fear which seems to stay constant in the relations between people and management is the introduction of new technologies. In fact, one of the primary responsibilities of the human resource function is to integrate new technology into the company without upsetting people. Again, people are most afraid of what they don't know about, so be open and up-front above all else. With the introduction of robots, automation and bar coding, the factory of the future will be highly technologically oriented. Job security becomes the number one concern of people and the problem in most need of being addressed. People need to be assured that their jobs will not be eliminated. There will certainly be different kinds of jobs and the company should provide education and training for any transition.

All of the above ideas must be implemented to smooth the transition, but, once again, attitude is the most crucial factor. If the changes and even the techniques to smooth the way for the changes are put into place without the involvement of people who are empowered to make their own choices, then the integration of any new technology or idea will be strongly resisted. People begin to lose touch (sometimes literally because of automation) with their jobs and the results can be lessened motivation, powerlessness and resentment.

As we have said all along, the time has come to get rid of the attitude which says that workers have no brains and that management knows what is best for them. Despite what Frederick Taylor may have learned from his time-motion studies about speeding up work, more recent psychological studies show that people who are deprived of a say in their work display the same characteristics mentioned above — lessened motivation, powerlessness and resentment. We agree with Michael Piori, professor of economics at the Massachusetts Institute of Technology who was reported in a recent issue of ***Managing Automation*** to believe that every person in a company should be given training and education in "the conceptual understanding of the manufacturing process." (***Managing Automation***, June 1989, p. 69.) We have advocated this all along as shown by our education and training triangle below:

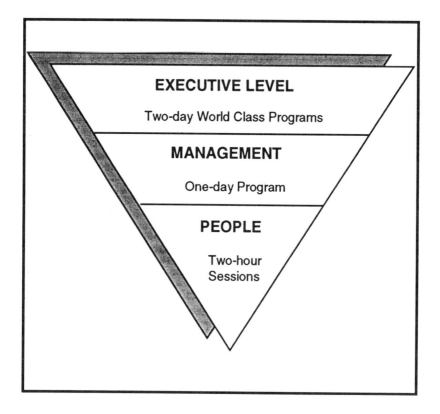

People who understand why they are doing work in a particular way are better able to figure out how to make the work more productive.

TECHNOLOGY AND PRODUCTIVITY IN THE OFFICE

Companies are finding that one fertile area for productivity improvements can be found in the office environment. Bringing in new and smarter office equipment, however, is not always the answer. Office automation often only produces more paperwork. Some companies think that getting rid of clerks and typists will improve productivity. Unfortunately, this only moves clerical tasks up to an already burdened next level.

The best method of gaining productivity improvements in the office is to use the same people involvement/empowerment program here as you would on the factory floor. The principles are still the same. The people on "the front lines" are the ones best able to find areas of improvement. Two areas to which teams should pay the most attention are:

---

1   **Evaluate all paperwork. Ask the question "Why?" five times. Can we eliminate, reduce or consolidate forms, memos, letters, etc.?**

2   **Observe lines of authority. Can we delegate more responsibility to lower levels of the organization?**

One of the biggest attitude problems we need to overcome in the office is that productivity improvement is not that important to the bottom line of the company. Bureau of Labor Statistics, however, show that productivity in the office in recent years has either declined or moved forward at an infinitesimal rate. Meanwhile, competition in the global marketplace has leaped ahead in this area.

QUALITY AND PRODUCTIVITY IMPROVEMENTS

Quality improvements begin with creating a positive environment where people are involved and empowered to work together with management in the belief that all things are possible. It doesn't matter what type of issue a team is working on, quality should always be part of the team's job. Some suggestions on how to get people to "own" quality are as follows:

- **Communicate throughout the workplace that the company expects 100 percent quality and nothing less.**

- **Focus your attention on the point where help is needed the most and then try to export the learning process throughout the company.**

- **Embrace quality yourself.**

- **Question people about what they are doing and encourage them to ask the question "why?" five times before they become satisfied with the answer.**

- **Establish a baseline from which to measure performance. Prominently display and discuss performance data.**

- **Adhere to these points daily in order to eliminate the "Quality Zone" syndrome.**

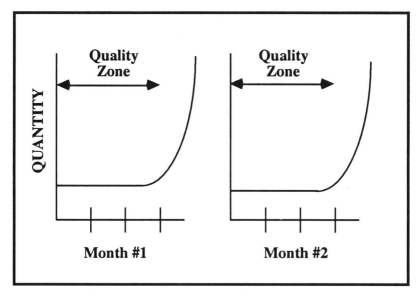

THE QUALITY ZONE SYNDROME — During the first three weeks of a typical month, we are concerned about quality. As soon as the fourth week starts, we change and become more concerned with quantity and shipments. The Quality Zone Syndrome was developed and demonstrated in quality programs by Phil Stang, Pro-Tech vice president.

John Wallace, CEO of the Wallace Co. which recently won the Malcolm Baldrige Quality Award, was quoted in *USA Today* as saying that showing total commitment on your own part was the best way to get people to buy into quality. He noted that letting associates give their input is the second most important part of the process. He firmly believes that if you present the facts to people and give them responsibility and authority, they will find the best solution. In the same article, Fred Smith, CEO of Federal Express (another Baldrige winner) said that the first time you accept less than 100% customer satisfaction after making the commitment to quality, you are heading backwards.

Now that we have an excellent idea of how to implement the change process, it is time that we look ahead to ways to develop skills in the areas of problem solving and decision analysis. The next chapter focuses on team approaches to these areas, approaches which we have found to be highly effective in every industry in which we have employed them.

Chapter Five

TEAM
SELECTION
CRITERIA

TEAM
SELECTION
CRITERIA

Team building proceeds, of course, with the selection of members to participate. We recommend that people not be selected by management. Every effort, via education, should be made to encourage people to volunteer. Ideally, total involvement is the best approach but we must temper this view with reality and base team involvement on the specific talent requirements needed by each team. One way to build a pool of talented potential team members is to have volunteer programs which allow people to work together on subjects to which they feel they can make the best contribution. Some programs may be mandatory in order for management to accomplish their goals. This may necessitate preselecting (identifying) people who would be the best candidates.

A pitfall to avoid when preselecting team members is labeling a worker as "uncooperative" because he or she does not want to be on a team. For example, at a company using an approach where teams were expected to meet on their time and not company time, an unhappy atmosphere was created. One worker made it clear that when she was at the company, she would always give eight hours of hard work. She couldn't provide any more because when she went home, she had to keep the books for her husband's business. Also remember that other meetings in an employee's personal life may preclude them from having extra time to devote to serving on a team. The happiness of the person serving on the team precludes all other considerations.

Elmer Miller, vice president of operations and general manager of the Caval Tool Division of Chromalloy Gas Turbine Corp., sent out the memo below when his company introduced Total Quality Management and people involvement into the workplace.

To: **All Caval Employees**
From: **Elmer Miller**
Subject: **Total Quality Management**

The growth of Caval Tool and the pressures of a rapidly changing business arena require us to challenge the way we manage our company's resources and to explore every opportunity to focus all our efforts toward continuous improvement.

Change makes many of us uncomfortable. Yet the customers we work for are driving us to change: to be faster and more accurate with the work we do for them. We may never be totally comfortable with change but we can and must learn to control it rather than feel victimized by it.

New concepts of management and methods of manufacturing are being explored and employed successfully by many of the global companies we compete with. Many of them are using a concept called Total Quality Management (TQM).

Total Quality Management (TQM) employs the concepts of employee involvement. Quite simply it promotes the old adage that two heads are better than one. That we can improve our competitiveness in the marketplace, more rapidly, if we work collectively rather than if we work separately.

Employee involvement exists in one form or another in every outstanding company. It uses specific tools and techniques that are different from those we are used to.

To introduce us to these tools and to help us employ these concepts, we will require outside assistance. Wayne Douchkoff from Pro-Tech will guide us through the implementation of this process.

We will start with four teams involving approximately 30 employees from different departments of our company. I will add teams as the year progresses and continue to do so, such that by the end of 1992, every employee of Caval Tool will be on an improvement team.

> In the near future you will attend a TQM
> education session that will provide additional
> insight into this improvement process. Some of
> you will be asked to participate in one of the
> first four teams and you will receive additional
> training in Team Problem Solving. Everyone
> will participate as more teams are added.
>
> I sincerely ask for your support and patience as
> we begin this worthwhile journey toward Total
> Quality Management.

Miller's memo is forthright. It discussed the difficult issues as well as the benefits to be derived from the program. We think this is the way every people involvement/empowerment should begin.

GETTING PEOPLE INVOLVEMENT

Volunteers should be chosen based on the specific talents a team may need. Volunteers are very helpful in a people involvement/ empowerment program because of the great enthusiasm they bring. Nothing dampens that enthusiasm more quickly than not being used once the team begins to function. A company should consider hand-picking if there are indications that the pool of volunteers is too large and covers more than the initial scope of the program. The most difficult problem occurs when a company needs a key person, such as a set-up person, to be a team member, but this person does not volunteer. You will have to make a special effort to convince this person of his or her importance to the team. Remember: You can attract more bees with honey than vinegar.

The composition of a team should be 50% hourly labor and 50% management. Certainly, you need people on the team with expertise. You also need people with little knowledge but with the ability to never be satisfied. There is something to say for "naive" members, the ones who ask all the seemingly "dumb" questions.

Our recommendation is that you ask for volunteers after you have told employees the number of teams you will start with and their size. Advise everybody that if too many people volunteer, they may not be used immediately, but will be asked to serve on future teams as they are formed. Instruct personnel that there are two types of teams — specific tasks and functional. Teams oriented toward specific tasks hit the problem, solve it and then disband. Such teams have shorter lives and provide participation more readily than functional teams. If, when using this process, a key person does not volunteer, a member of the steering committee may contact that person and ask them to join a team.

THE STRUCTURE OF PEOPLE INVOLVEMENT/EMPOWERMENT PROGRAMS

People involvement/empowerment programs structurally consist of a steering committee which oversees the empowerment process and which guides the teams that carry out the work. In between is the facilitator and/or team leader whose job it is to keep the lines of communication open between the two primary structures of the process. It is possible to have a consultant act as a facilitator. The role is to provide assistance and direct guidance to the team leader. This can consist of aiding in the following ways:

- Provide administrative assistance.

- Implement education/training.

- Assist in providing guidance in interpersonal dealings with team members.

- Obtain resources in order to achieve results.

The structures discussed above are depicted in the diagram below:

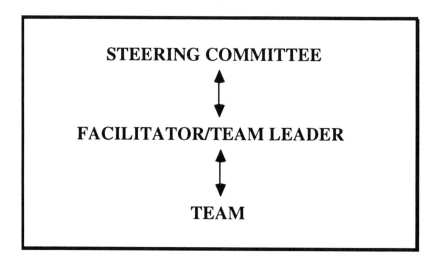

The first step in team-building is to form a steering committee. The steering committee should be an interdepartmental team whose job it is to provide resources and ensure continuous improvement. The steering committee should consist of people from the following areas:

- **Representatives from top management.**
- **Middle management.**
- **Supervisors.**
- **Hourly workers.**
- **Union representation.**

We recommend a maximum of nine people on this committee. Larger groups become misdirected or stagnant. The committee's directives are the same ones that are taught to managers in Business 101—planning, organizing, staffing, controlling and directing. During the **planning** stage, the steering committee should be discussing these questions:

- How many teams should we start out with?
- Where are they coming from?
- When are they going to meet?
- What resources do they need? Dollars, equipment, education/training, travel, etc.

STEERING COMMITTEE

We have determined from our experience with numerous clients in a number of industries that an effective steering committee has similar characteristics. First of all it should be staffed by people who are not afraid of change. Then, it should have the following roles in a people involvement/empowerment program:

- **Provide resources and accountability.**
- **Assure that plans and action are consistent with goals.**
- **Make policy.**
- **Review progress.**
- **Resolve conflicts.**
- **Demonstrate interest and commitment.**

The most important task of the steering committee is to form teams. Project teams, as the name implies, coalesce around certain projects brought to attention by the steering committee. In a typical implementation, we recommend four to five teams of 8-10 people. Trying to put all of a company's employees on a team is probably too much to handle at the beginning, except in smaller companies. On the other hand, one team is too few. A question we are often asked is when to add more teams. We say that when the initial teams are functioning well, it's time to add more. Additional teams may be salted with people from the initial teams. In fact, we strongly recommend that the first teams consist of people who have good interpersonal skills, people who will eventually make good team leaders on their own team.

The steering committee must also **organize** teams so that they know their mission. Each team should develop a charter which clearly states aims and goals. They are assisted in this task by the introductory training they received. The draft charter is then presented to the steering committee for approval. This approach builds a sense of ownership within the team while the committee is able to ensure consistency of purpose. We recommend that you let individual teams decide what is the most important problem within guidelines set by the steering committee. The charter, for example, could simply be to reduce set-up time on Machine #2.

Another task of the steering committee is to **staff** the teams. The general rule is that a team should have five to nine members and that for every salaried or management person, there should be an hourly worker. When a team gets above nine people, there is a tendency for one or two people to do all the talking and everybody else to listen. We don't want to see this. It defeats the whole purpose of a team which is to have people both listen and talk. Don't be afraid to ask top management to be on a team. However, it is suggested that management not be part of the team at the outset. Not until support has been demonstrated by management and results are being achieved should management be on teams.

At that point they should first be visible at meetings but should not participate immediately. The team must be allowed to open itself up to management. It would be a good idea to let them and others find out what it's like to work together. In fact, every employee, including members of the steering committee, should be on a team at some point in time. Teams should also represent a good cross-section of the company. The diagram below shows one possible team configuration:

	Controller/VP Finance	Production Planning Mgr	Purchasing Manager	Quality Supervisor	Master Production Planner	Set-Up Person	Operator	Material Handler
Top Management	X							
Middle Management		X	X					
Supervisors				X				
Hourly						X	X	X	X

Possible Team Configuration

The steering committee also has the responsibility of **monitoring** the teams. This means that once every four to eight weeks the individual team leaders must give a ten-minute presentation to the committee. In this report, the team and/or leader must tell what they have accomplished in the last month by presenting the team fishbone and team measurements.

It is the steering committee's function to **guide** the team's progress. After hearing its periodic report, the committee should decide whether the team is on track and whether they are achieving the goals of the charter. If they aren't, then the steering committee will have to find out why and help the team get back on track.

RULES FOR TEAM OPERATION

The rules or plans of action of a team is to work within the guidelines of the steering committee. The steering committee is a catalyst. It defines what people involvement/empowerment means to the company, reviews projects, provides resources and guides the overall problem solving effort. Another way to put this is to say that the steering committee creates the culture for change and maintains that environment.

If the steering committee is the strategy maker, then the team finds ways to implement that strategy. Any team, then, really has only one overall mandate — investigate symptoms, identify the causes of problems, identify the means to solve the problem and implement them.

Selecting team members with fresh insight is one way to break down existing barriers in your company. Another way is to expose teams to the full range of problems. The idea behind teamwork is to expand the base of experience, so that no one team, for example, becomes known as the team responsible for quality. Quality is everybody's responsibility. Thus, you should make sure that quality problems are addressed on all teams.

Another way to break down barriers and maintain freshness is to adopt an open-door policy. At one of our client's, L'Oréal Cosmetics (Cosmair), for example, there were gray doors separating the office from the factory floor. One of the first activities of the team at the plant was to create an environment where the doors were no longer a barrier. Their rationale was that open doors create an environment for open minds.

At the same Cosmair plant, Gerry Price, then vice president of manufacturing, volunteered to work two days a month on the production line. And he did, from 7:30 a.m. to 3:30 p.m., with no phone calls allowed and only scheduled breaks and lunch time. He was heard to remark after the first day that "this is hard work." He admitted to a profound change in his views. Needless to say, line workers were far more apt to listen to a vice president who had worked in the trenches. Again, this is the type of management player you want on your team. Somebody willing to get their hands dirty.

Team members should have the ability to question and to be open coupled with the qualities of energy, excitement and experience. Team members must be given the proper decision-making authority and responsibility to make changes. Since your teams will ideally have an equal number of hourly workers and management, you will have to show workers that you mean what you say. Giving hourly workers equal representation, of course, says more than mere words. We have found this technique to be particularly effective in encouraging participation and overcoming workers' fears in the face of management. In short, the same non-adversarial approach which determines better supplier relationships should also determine the relationship between management and hourly workers.

At Cosmair, for instance, one worker who initially spoke out against certain facets of JIT was intentionally picked to be on a team. At first, he could not understand why and did not participate while attending meetings. But, in one meeting, the team began talking about reducing set-up time. This worker then got up and came up with an idea for eliminating wasteful activities. At the end of the meeting, he told us he now understood why he was on the team. He is now an enthusiastic supporter of change.

TEAM RULES AND OBJECTIVES

There are inherent problems with teams. Whenever a lot of cooks are stirring the broth, there will be arguments over what ingredients are best. How do you form and manage a team in which you reap the benefits of a diverse group while not stifling individual creativity? How can Purchasing sit down with Marketing, Engineering, Production and Quality and come up with integrated solutions? How do you create a team?

The answer comes in four parts. One, you need to establish ground rules, goals, objectives and a sense of direction. Two, you need to educate and train all levels of your company in people involvement/empowerment as the means to attain World Class Status. Three, you must teach teams how to administer the formation and implementation of the action plans. Four, you must initiate program reviews and provide ongoing support. All of these parts are the work of the steering committee and teams tackling problems together. They are done within your plant through the cooperation of different departments and outside your plant through the creation of a partnership with your suppliers.

Let's look first at the establishment of rules and objectives. The overall goals of teams are the same as those we have repeatedly emphasized for all facets of people involvement/empowerment. The company must infuse a sense of vision, responsibility, authority and accountability in the group which gathers to work on a task. We must move toward a manufacturing environment in which the previously separate areas merge. In other words, people involvement/empowerment is a process of fusion, rather than fission. Energy is created as different departments work closer and closer together, as the barriers between them slowly break down, just as our sun creates energy by fusing hydrogen atoms into ones of helium. In the process of fusion, your company will move from ignorance and confusion about people involvement/empowerment to the adoption of a World Class mind-set.

ORGANIZING FOR TEAMWORK

As for the amount of time which should be devoted to team meetings, we recommend that the time spent in a meeting be one or one and a half hours per week. We also expect each team member to spend the same amount of time outside the team meeting doing the assignments for which they volunteered. Team members should expect assignments at every team meeting. If the assignment is to collect data, the team member should organize that data for review by the team. Pareto charts, histograms, process flow charts, etc. may be required. The team member should come to the next meeting ready to share information, to brainstorm and decide what to do next, to make new assignments and then to adjourn and start working on them in preparation for the next team meeting.

So, if a team spends one and a half hours in a meeting and one and a half hours collecting data or performing their assignments, does that mean that they are working three hours a week on company time? Yes, it most definitely does. Remember that you are investing in the future of your company. If you need to ask people to work overtime to get all the work done, then that is a small price to pay, given the documented benefits of people involvement/empowerment.

RESERVING TIME TO MEET

One more point about team meeting times: If you have two shifts, then plan the meeting at the shift change in order to include employees from both shifts. That way, each shift only loses a half hour. For example, if the shift change is at 4 p.m., then the meeting should begin at 3:30 p.m. and end at 4:30 p.m. If there are three shifts, then it will be necessary to rotate the meeting times or to have separate teams for each shift. The separate teams would work on different problems. They would all have to abide by one rule as well. That rule would state that they have an obligation to talk to the other shift employees and pass ideas back and forth.

RULES TO PLAY BY

For teams to function effectively, certain rules must be enforced. Here is a list of rules which our clients have found helpful:

- **Each team has three roles: (1) Solving problems, (2) Implementing solutions, and (3) Measuring and reporting results.**

- **Teams should pick a leader they trust and one they feel can best help the team meet its objectives.**

- A scribe for each team is also required. Team members should also select this person. Scribes can capture the activities and accomplishments of the team.

- Consistent standards for reporting should be established for all teams to follow.

- The roles of the facilitator/leader are to be an administrator, communicator and a team aid who obtains resources and who observes, listens, questions and acts to assist the team in obtaining results.

- Teams must follow a step-by-step set of procedures in their problem solving activities.

- Meetings should normally last 60 minutes and they should stop and start on time.

- Team leaders should keep the team together by keeping the team focused on the task at hand.

- Team members should attend all meetings, be on time, receive no messages and never walk out.

- Team members should also be helpful to other team members and keep the leader informed.

- **The team has the responsibility of following the agenda, participating by doing assignments and supporting the decision making process.**

KEEPING TEAM MEMBER INTEREST

People's interest begins with top management's commitment to a culture that accepts change. This is where teamwork gets the energy to sustain itself. Teamwork breeds interest. Management needs to commit itself to granting people the time to solve problems. It should also allow the creative solution of problems in an environment where there is no harassment from management. Management should only provide direction and focus; it should never rule by edict. Maintaining momentum in a people involvement/empowerment program can be accomplished by focusing on the following:

- **Promotion of success.**
- **Establishing objectives which challenge the team to achieve the desired results.**

One of the problems faced by a company that is implementing a people involvement/empowerment program is that it replaces practices of the past. The best way to start anew is to reinforce past accomplishments and ask people how they can improve on them. You will have to challenge the attitude that this is just another program and it, too, will pass. Tell your people that improvement is everybody's job and that all solutions are invented here. On the other hand, tell them not to be afraid to look elsewhere so they can learn from the success of others. If people "own" the program, there should be little or no problem in keeping involvement and interest high.

Do not insist that results occur right away. We have a rule that we call the "50/50% of Achievement Rule." It says that we should progress slowly in a step-by-step process. First, work to attain improvements that get you 50 percent of the way to your goal; then reestablish your target to get another 50 percent of the way to your goal; and then another 50 percent; and so on and so on until your ultimate goal is reached. This process is far superior to the "all or nothing" rule because improvements are real and sustainable.

CROSS-FERTILIZATION TEAMS

Teams need to be aware of the activities of other teams in the company. This cross-fertilization and coordination of efforts makes sure that efforts are not being duplicated. These efforts and activities should be coordinated through the area's supervisor who can understand and buy into what people are doing.

In the next chapter, we will take a look at how to take the members which have been selected and develop their skills in problem solving and decision analysis.

Chapter Six

DEVELOPING SKILLS: PROBLEM SOLVING AND DECISION ANALYSIS

DEVELOPING SKILLS: PROBLEM SOLVING AND DECISION ANALYSIS

The major problem companies have with problem solving is an inability to define the process and the characteristics to be studied. We don't know how to find the real causes of problems. This is because the responsibility for problem solving is poorly defined by management. Most systems are inadequate or misunderstood and the approaches to problem solving are unstructured.

Companies are also guilty of attacking the whole problem instead of sizing up the problem and then attacking its parts. Management tends to treat symptoms and not eliminate the causes. Management often focuses on short-term solutions which miss treating the real cause of a problem. Too often, companies also expect and even reward "Big Gains" and individual achievement. Sustained improvement comes only with continuous small gains. The baseball team that wins the World Series is the team that hits singles, not home runs.

Again, it is the delegation of responsibility and authority to the level where the problem can best be solved which is so critical to success. Recently at Loran, for example, we saw just how powerful this delegation of problem solving can be.

Loran, as mentioned earlier, manufactures cassettes. For one of its customers, Ford Motor Co., it manufactures a tape cassette and then stamps a number in sequence on the outside. This stamping operation was done after the magnetic tape was wound on to the cassette. Then an operator manipulated a semi-automatic numbering machine. This caused a number of problems as the inking of the pad tended to be sloppy and product would get damaged. Production time was also lost cleaning the ink off the pad, equipment and the floor.

A team started to look into the problem. An engineer on the team suggested purchasing an automated ink jet printer. Some time was then spent by the team on justifying the purchase of this $7,000 printer. The team determined that they could get a payback in seven to eight months. Everything looked good until a production line worker asked the most obvious, the most simple and the most important question of all: Why do we need the serial number? The answer, of course, was that Ford required it. The next smart idea: Why don't we ask Ford?

To come to the point, Ford no longer required the serial number and, in fact, hadn't for a long while.

We simply love coming across these examples of people who deal with day-to-day operations asking the questions they were told were "dumb," but which are, in fact, the smartest questions that can be asked. Remember what your grade school teachers used to say: The only dumb question is the one that doesn't get asked.

OUR PROBLEM SOLVING PROCESS

Once a team identifies a problem through an analysis of the data which has been collected, it must seek solutions. Over the years, we have developed a four-step problem solving process. We recommend the four-step process in all cases except those which involve immediately obvious and simple solutions. Another exception might be granted to a situation where a team is faced with numerous problems. They may gain some "breathing room" by solving critical problems in a "quick and dirty" manner.

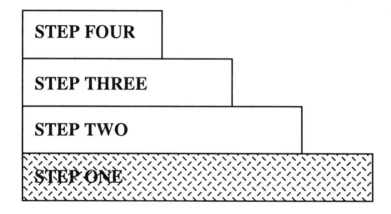

NAME THE PROBLEM

The first step for the team is to use the form in Figure 1 which is divided into three columns with the following headings:

- Symptoms.
- Possible causes.
- Verified root causes.

In the first column, the team writes down the symptom from which the company is suffering and that they will attempt to remedy. The key element here is that what we formerly labeled a problem was in reality a symptom. Examples are late deliveries of tools, part shortages, unhappy customers, line-up problems, maintenance problems, etc. Symptoms consist of many causes, each of which is a problem to be solved by the group once it is verified.

Figure 1

Symptom	Possible Causes	Verified Root Causes
Terrible-tasting coffee Too dark		

In the second column, the team lists all of the possible reasons why a particular symptom could be occurring, as shown in Figure 2. These two columns should be able to be completed in a one-hour meeting.

Figure 2

Symptom	Possible Causes	Verified Root Causes
Terrible-tasting coffee Too dark	Too much coffee Water is hard Strong blend	

Filling in the third column, in which the team must decide what are the vital few, or root causes, is the most difficult part. The team must find the two or three causes which would make most of the symptoms disappear if those causes were attacked and eliminated.

This stage can require as little as a week or month to complete, depending on the time allotted to problem solving. The team leader/facilitator must make assignments for each possible cause indicated in the second column. Team members then have to go out and do research on the factory floor and wherever else to collect data and talk to the people who are involved. The data gathering step may not be necessary if data is already being collected and put into a Pareto format. Then, the team members are expected to come back to the meeting and compare data. This process must continue until they are able to identify a few root causes.

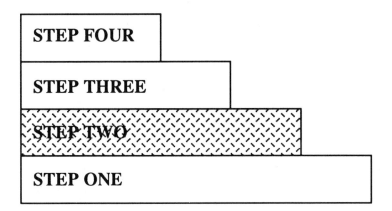

FIND A WAY

Next the team must find **ways** to **eliminate** or **reduce** each of these root causes. The key words here are "ways," "eliminate" and "reduce." We need to look beyond the first solution which comes to mind and we must be sure that each solution positively "kills" the problem. This process is known as "killing snakes" at Trinity Industries, Inc. Daryl Collings, the production control manager, was instrumental in using this process to identify and eliminate the root causes of poor schedule attainment. By finding ways to eliminate lack of material, machinery breakdowns, etc., Trinity was able to attain levels of greater than 90 percent performance to schedule at several locations. But, as part of a continuous improvement process, they maintain the use of this problem solving technique to strive toward 100 percent. Teams should be instructed to try and eliminate problems. Every problem, however, does not lend itself to elimination. A focused team should be able to implement substantial reductions for problems which can't be eliminated. One example which comes to mind is off-shore supplier lead-times.

The continuous improvement process begins when the team leader/facilitator fills out the top of the form below for each problem, or Verified Root Cause:

MUST FIND **WAYS** TO **ELIMINATE**	
(Verified Root Cause)	
	Cost of Each Solution
Solution #1: _____	#1
Solution #2: _____	#2
Solution #3: _____	#3
Solution #4: _____	#4
Solution #5: _____	#5
NEXT STEP = EXECUTE **WHO** _____ **WHEN** _____	

Then the leader/facilitator points to the first problem, Verified Root Cause #1, and asks the team members for potential ways to eliminate the problem. We strongly recommend using The Formal Brainstorming process as the fastest approach. The leader/facilitator then directs a discussion of each possible solution. He or she does not list a second solution until the team is reasonably sure that the first solution will work.

The first solution will often suggest that the company either spend money, buy equipment or hire people. The second solution is more difficult to come up with. When a second solution has been put forward, the leader/facilitator does not ask for a third solution until the team is, once again, reasonably sure that Solution #2 will eliminate the root cause. The leader/facilitator continues this same procedure for the third, fourth and fifth solutions. We recommend five solutions as a rule of thumb, but don't force five if there are only four solutions. Don't study a problem to death.

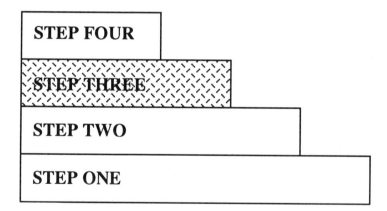

ASSIGN COSTS

Step three is relatively straight-forward. Take each of the solutions for a particular root cause and assign a cost to it in terms of people, machines and materials. Put this dollar amount in the appropriate space on the form. After this is done, it is obvious which solution to implement—the one with the *lowest cost* since the team is already reasonably sure that all the solutions will eliminate the root cause and the problem. The team must not only present how much a solution will cost, but also predict the benefit. This method then allows the team to determine that the lowest cost solution may not always be the best solution. We must take into consideration the time required to execute the solution. Sometimes, time is of the essence and a minimal cost difference may be worth the quicker resolution.

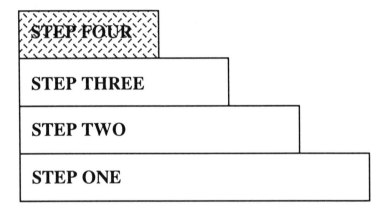

EXECUTE THE PLAN

From our experience, we have found it necessary to add an execution step to this problem solving technique. Sometimes, teams believe that going through the three previous steps automatically makes the problem disappear. Or, they believe that their job is finished and now it is up to someone else to implement the solution. We advocate that the team be empowered with the *responsibility* and *authority* to implement its own solutions. If the problem doesn't go away, then the team must make another attempt to solve the problem.

We refer you to the action process steps identified in the next chapter for more information. Also, remember that in order to ensure that the cause of a problem is eliminated, measurements must be taken in an on-going program as described in Chapter Eight.

This four-step process can also be used to develop a presentation to top management. Now a team can say: We've looked at the symptoms. We identified these possible causes and then we verified these three as the roots of the problem. We've come up with five ways to eliminate each problem. This is the one with the lowest cost. This is the one we are going to implement. By following this process, the team will have a better chance of having management release funds needed for implementation.

Does this problem solving process work? We've been involved in many instances where it absolutely does. At one foundry, we facilitated a set-up team tackling the problem of porosity in castings. The company was currently scrapping three castings per month. The team went through the steps above and came up with six solutions. The first cost $100,000. The sixth cost $150 per year. Was it good a solution? It was good enough so that in the last nine months, the company has not scrapped any castings. Did the team "kill" the problem? Yes, absolutely.

FISHBONE DIAGRAMS

Tom Peters, at a recent talk, told the assembled businesspeople that if companies did not know how to do fishbone diagrams by

1991, they would be educationally deficient. Fishbones are tremendous brainstorming tools. We advise clients to put the fishbone diagram on a "wipe-off" board in the work area. Then, people can list possible cause underneath each category. We do ask that people put their name down in case the team has more questions to ask. Another way is to make one list of all the causes and then categorize each item under the six headings.

As the cause and effect (fishbone) diagram on the facing page shows, the intent is to identify a problem and its possible causes and then to note which causes are being worked on and which are done. We instruct teams to put parentheses "( )" around what the team is currently working on and to put a dot next to the item when it is finished. This makes the diagram a great visual reminder of progress as well as what specific cause they are working on at the moment.

One variation on the fishbone idea is to put the diagram on a 4' x 8' sheet of board. Other employees are encouraged to add possible causes, not identified by the team, by sticking "Post-it" notes on the board under the appropriate heading. It is very possible that the person with the ideal solution is not a team member. This method allows that person to make a contribution.

Fishbones are also valuable for the following reasons:

- **Focus team on specific issues.**
- **Identify possible causes of a problem.**
- **Relate causes to effect.**
- **Analyze all possible causes of a problem.**
- **Trace the symptoms of causes.**
- **Break problems into their smallest parts.**

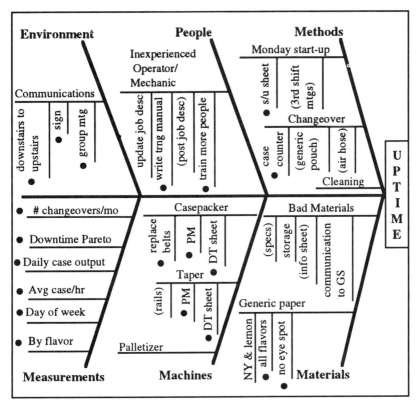

Fishbone Diagram

Fishbone diagrams make excellent one-page memos. Send a diagram like the above and top management instantly knows what is being done. In fact, we recommend that fishbones be a part of the ten-minute presentations that teams should make to a steering committee every month. In each of these presentations, the team leader/facilitator should first put up a measurement graph and talk about it. It should show, for example, how something has decreased (or increased) over the past month. Then, the team leader/facilitator should put up a fishbone diagram and explain to the steering committee what the team is doing now and what has been completed. Lastly, the team leader/facilitator should tell the committee how the team went through the four-step process for problem solving in order to obtain viable solutions. This makes a far more effective presentation than someone reading the minutes of the previous month's meetings as well as being much more efficient and timely.

The intent of a fishbone is to identify a problem and its possible causes and then to note which causes are being worked on and which are done. It is not so important where you place the problem on the fishbone as it is to identify the problem and causes. If you spend too much time deciding what goes where, you could contract the dreaded disease of "paralysis through analysis." We warn you not to study a plan to death. Problem solving is more than identification; it is action. It is taking the necessary steps to correct a deviation from the norm.

CORRECTION STEPS FOR DEVIATION

Once the problem is identified, then we are ready to correct the deviation using these steps:

- Develop specific goals and have the right tools.
- Identify exactly what is out of control.
    Accumulate data (reports)
    Summarize data on one sheet of paper
    Chart data so it is understandable to the layperson and the operator
- Discuss a solution.
    Break diagnosis into manageable units
    Analyze data
    Define problem and brainstorm

• Initiate action.
    Develop a plan for new standards
    Utilize feedback
    Monitor
    Establish control so action remains
            consistent with overall process
            and timely completion (target
            date)

PROBLEM SOLVING GUIDELINE QUESTIONS

The following six guidelines, adopted from **Set-Up Reduction: Saving Dollars with Common Sense** (Jerry W. Claunch, Philip D. Stang, PT Publications, Inc., Palm Beach Gardens, FL) use set-up reduction as an example of one area a team will tackle. Similar checklists, to be developed by a team or outside consultants, will help a company begin the problem solving process necessary for a successful people involvement/empowerment program. Please note that although the questions relate to manufacturing, they can be flavored to address administrative duties and tasks.

GUIDELINE #1: MATERIAL

Use of better materials, or use of present materials in more efficient ways, can greatly improve set-up time.

__ Could a less expensive material be used which would function as well?

__ Does the material arrive at the work center in suitable condition for use?

__ Could the supplier or previous work center do additional work on the material to make it better suited for use?

__ Is the material clean enough for use?

__ Is the material ordered in quantities or sizes that facilitate the most efficient use of set-up time?

__ Would a more expensive material, which was easier to process, result in a saving?

__ Can the product design be changed to eliminate material requiring lengthy or costly set-ups?

__ Is it possible to reduce the number of materials by standardizing product designs?

__ Are provisions in place for segregation of different material cuttings to assure maximum return?

__ If a more consistent grade of material was used, would it be possible to gain better control of set-up operations necessary for processing the material?

GUIDELINE #2: MATERIAL HANDLING and TRANSPORT OF MATERIAL

Material handling is not only the movement of material from work center to work center. It includes the movement of material at the work center as well. Better material handling can improve housekeeping, simplify operations and improve quality, all of which will greatly impact set-up reduction.

__ Should operators perform material handling functions?

__ Should special racks or trays be developed to improve handling time and to decrease the amount of damage done to material?

__ With respect to the work center, where should incoming and outgoing material be located?

__ Can work centers which do successive steps of the process be moved closer together to improve material handling?

__ Is the size of the container which is used to transport material suitable for the size or quantity of material needed?

__ Can the container be designed to make the material more accessible?

__ Can material be handled during an idle period of the operation?

__ Is the storage area efficiently located?

__ Can waist-high material containers be used at work centers?

__ Is it possible to combine operations at a work center to reduce material handling?

GUIDELINE #3: SET-UP AND PUT AWAY

This checklist focuses on who is the best person to perform the set-up activity.

__ How is the job assigned to the operator?

__ What possibilities for delays occur at the storeroom?

__ If the operator performs the set-up, would there be any gains if it was done by a trained set-up person?

__ Is the work center orderly so that tools can be found quickly?

__ Are the tools used in the set-up adequate?

__ Is the machine in proper working condition?

__ Is the workplace layout an effective one? Or, can a more efficient way be found to arrange work centers?

__ Is the material properly positioned?

__ Are the first few pieces produced checked by anyone other than the operator?

__ How is the material supply replenished?

__ If a number of miscellaneous jobs are done, can they be grouped together to eliminate some set-up elements?

__ Are benches and tables of the proper height and design?

__ Who checks the fluid levels of the equipment and performs other preventive maintenance?

__ Are tools transferred from one shift or worker to another without undue loss of time?

__ Could guides be used to position parts more accurately?

__ Do all operators and set-up people use the same tools?

__ Do all operators and set-up people use the same procedure?

__ Are proper measuring instruments provided for precision work and are they calibrated on a regular schedule?

__ Would it be feasible to hang tools on springs overhead?

__ Does the set-up person need to reach and could this distance be shortened?

__ Does the set-up person need to walk away from the work center? Could this be eliminated?

__ Will ratchet, spiral or power tools save time?

GUIDELINE #4: MACHINERY

This guideline's focus is the equipment which is directly used to perform the operation.

__ Are machines checked on a regular schedule to insure good condition?

__ Are machines properly powered with the right type of motor?

__ Is this particular machine best suited to the job at hand?

__ Could the machine be outfitted or adapted to perform better or to allow for easier change-over?

GUIDELINE #5: WORKING CONDITIONS

This is not only a set-up issue. Working conditions are serious deterrents to the performance of set-ups. Eliminating poor conditions can help reduce set-up time or work effort in correlation with other factors to reduce activity time.

__ Is lighting uniform and sufficient at all times?

__ Have glare and reflections been eliminated at the work center?

__ Is the proper temperature maintained for maximum productivity?

__ Is ventilation good?

__ Are safety factors duly emphasized?

__ Are tools and motor drives properly guarded?

__ Is wooden equipment, such as work benches, in good condition and free of splinters?

__ Is the floor free of debris and smooth, but not slippery?

__ Is the set-up person's clothing safe and comfortable?

__ Can noisy conditions be quieted?

__ Is the area clean?

GUIDELINE #6: GENERAL CONSIDERA- TIONS

__ Are adequate performance records maintained?

__ Are new set-up people properly introduced to their surroundings and are sufficient instructions given to them?

__ Are failures to meet standard performance requirements investigated?

__ Are suggestions from workers encouraged?

__ Is the set-up being performed by the proper class of labor?

__ Is the set-up person physically suited for the job?

SETTING THE STAGE
FOR EMPLOYEE INVOLVEMENT

It should be clear by now that teams armed with problem solving techniques are the most effective way to reduce and then eliminate waste. Technical knowledge is valuable and necessary, but, as we have seen, so is the ability to get the best out of people by building a creative environment. Each part of the people involvement/ empowerment program is as critical as any other part. People issues need to be addressed. If they aren't, all the problem solving techniques in the world won't help a team. In the next chapter, we will take a look at how to run productive team meetings.

Chapter Seven

TEAM ADMINISTRATION: CONDUCTING TEAM MEETINGS AND PRESENTATIONS

TEAM ADMINISTRATION: CONDUCTING TEAM MEETINGS AND PRESENTATIONS

Teams can be made up of individuals from a number of disciplines within your company. Thus, when a team sets out to solve a problem, there are inputs from a number of diverse areas, each of which states how possible solutions will effect them. Hypotheses and plans of action are developed via a group process. This approach has been documented as producing more meaningful participation. Undoubtedly, participation and its effectiveness in generating suggestions is predicated on our need to be a part of a focused group as well as retain an individual identity.

The results of a team will be greater than the sum of efforts made by individuals. As we pointed out in another book, **Made In America** (PT Publications, Palm Beach Gardens, FL), a team can see internal and external interactive aspects of your company and the reverberations caused by actions in one department as they ripple through the company as a whole.

Only minimal expenditures are needed to improve communication, to involve the workforce in problem solving and decision-making, or to develop interdepartmental cooperation. Since direct labor works with management on teams, there is an opportunity for both to mutually explore theory (education) and practice techniques (training). With this level of cooperation, learning curves are accelerated, thus lowering total cost.

In effect, the creation of a company culture favoring team building fosters vision, responsibility, authority and accountability. The key to the creation of a framework of continuous improvement is teamwork. Just as farmers in rural sections of our country take a day to raise a barn for a neighbor, teamwork calls for action by all levels of your organization.

WHAT IS A TEAM?

One characteristic of the Far East which helps them achieve remarkable results is their sense of teamwork. It is certainly a lesson we can learn from. We must emphasize and reward teamwork in our companies. But, what exactly is a team? Some people confuse teams with consensus management or a slowly moving company that can't make a decision. The teams we advocate are quite the opposite. We define a team as the following:

TEAM (*noun*)—A group of people dedicated to a common goal who have learned to build on each other's strengths and to compensate for each other's weaknesses.

Everybody has pluses and minuses. All of us have different backgrounds and different acquired skills. Some of us are more expressive and natural leaders. Others are more analytically inclined and better at collecting and organizing data. Still others are more mechanically inclined. The point is that every hand is a helping hand.

We have to get rid of what we call the "hand grenade" mentality in which one person or department thinks it's doing well and that everybody else is doing poorly. In other words: "I'm O.K. and you're not!" We want to break down these kind of barriers to improvement and get departments like engineering and manufacturing to work with each other toward designing better products. We need to encourage people to talk with the maintenance department if there is a problem with the quality of products in order to recognize the impact one area has on another when it undertakes an action. We must encourage our people to begin helping each other. In reality, the "working" teams described here are better described as "hard-working" teams with a powerful orientation to getting results.

TEAM LEADERS AND SCRIBES — Their Roles

The definition of administration is 1) performance of duties and 2) guiding the execution of activities. The team leader's administrative role is to direct and focus team activities and to insure that management is informed of the progress of the team's efforts. The team leader plays a vital role in the functioning of the team. His or her qualities can make or break a team. We recommend that a team pick its own leader by consensus. He or she should not necessarily be a member of management. The most important quality a leader should have is strong interpersonal skills. A leader needs to keep the team focused on objectives by getting members to feel and participate as equals. A team leader should also be adept at delegating responsibility. Team members should not feel that the leader is the only person who can make decisions. Finally, the team leader needs to kindle the interest of people in order to get them to volunteer and contribute.

Every team should also have a team scribe. This person needs to have the ability to take notes on the activities of the team. The scribe should take meeting minutes and prepare an agenda before each meeting. The task of documenting the meeting should include a summary of all subjects discussed and any assignments made to team members. The scribe should also be involved in documenting savings realized by the team. This doesn't mean that the scribe is the only person responsible for measurements since that is the responsibility of the team as a whole. The team leader and members are also responsible for informing the scribe of any issues, problems or solutions which need to be noted in the minutes.

TRAINING AND EDUCATION

Education is learning the theory behind what you are doing; training is putting into practice what you have learned. Education must occur at all levels of a company. Contrary to traditional educational methods used by many companies where more time is spent teaching direct labor than management, we invert the educational pyramid as we have already shown in Chapter Four.

Top management receives more extensive education because without their understanding and commitment, the rest of your education and training program will go nowhere. It is an undeniable fact that workers look to their leaders for direction. A middle manager is far more apt to embrace people involvement/empowerment if she sees a vice president genuinely committed to it.

Training is a tool to help your business meet its objectives today and in the future. Your goal, then, is to provide a positive atmosphere which will stimulate employees to discuss theory, practices and alternatives. You should base training on job competency and focus it on creating greater cross-functional awareness. Training and education must become a way of life in your company. Some companies, for example, always have some structured activities for their workers whenever a line shuts down. We recommend that you use downtime to instruct employees in employing problem solving techniques, in performance measurements or in interpersonal skills. It's a way of life whose end result is to give workers the tools for continuous improvement.

The first priority in planning a training and education program in your plant is to assess needs and opportunities. We have developed a competency model which will assist you in defining where your company is proficient and deficient. You should use this

Competency Model for Determining Knowledge and Skill Requirements By Function

COMPETENCY AREAS	Marketing	Finance	Sales	Production	Quality	Purchasing	Planning	Traffic
TQM Principles	3	3	3	3	3	3	3	3
Set-up Reduction	1	2	1	3	3	3	3	1
Supplier Certification	2	1	2	3	3	3	3	3
SPC	1	1	1	3	3	3	3	2
Preventive Maint.	1	1	1	3	1	1	2	1
Value Analysis	1	1	1	3	3	3	3	2
Problem solving	3	3	3	3	3	3	3	3
MRP II	2	3	2	3	2	3	3	3

1. indicates a familiarity with subject
2. requires a working knowledge of field
3. requires expertise in area

model as a guide. The numbers indicate the necessary levels of expertise for each function and are specific to the company. By comparing the levels of expertise within your company to the desired levels in the chart, you can determine short-term and long-term objectives in your education and training program.

Once you have these objectives accurately developed, you can begin to develop a schedule of training and education which suits your particular needs. The following is a sample training and education program:

EDUCATION AND TRAINING
ACTIVITY PLAN

Activity	| Time Periods									
	1	2	3	4	5	6	7	8	9	10
Assess needs	x									
Evaluate competency	x	x								
Develop preliminary plan		x								
Prepare budget		x								
Obtain management support		x								
Develop steering committee	x									
Develop project team		x	x							
Outline course plan			x							
Develop program measurements			x							
Train the trainers			x							
Hold pilot model courses				x						
Schedule education courses *					x					
Schedule training courses					x					
Measure results					x	x	x	x	x	x
Measure TQM perf. results							x	x	x	x
Revise program as required								x	x	x

* SPC, Set-up Reduction, Supplier Certification

As for the course content itself, it should include the following approach for successful people involvement/empowerment:

> 1. **Principles and techniques.**
> 2. **How to study.**
> 3. **Objectives.**
> 4. **Focus on practical applications.**
> 5. **Case studies.**
> 6. **Historical and current perspectives.**
> 7. **Company differences.**
> 8. **Interface requirements.**

TEAM FACILITATION
>   — **Assigning Tasks to Get Results**
>   — **Understanding Behavioral Guidelines**
>   — **Administering Meetings**

The stage is set for implementing and managing the tasks which will lead to people involvement/empowerment. The Task Team Process begins with a needs and readiness assessment to evaluate the current status of the task team's area of inquiry and the opportunities which are present. This assessment should include the following actions:

> 1. **Create a business vision statement (objectives).**
> 2. **Structure organization for success.**
> 3. **Identify opportunities for improvement.**
> 4. **Identify existing and required skills inventory.**
> 5. **Assess climate/political environment.**
> 6. **Determine impact of existing company culture.**
> 7. **Develop plan to implement process.**

This will undoubtedly result in a long list of areas upon which to improve. The second step is to prioritize the list. The third step is to make a timetable which defines the tasks identified in the implementation plan. Each task must show its dependency on the completion of another task and schedule. Be sure to establish beginning and end dates. We have found that without a start date, tasks may not be completed on time.

Once the tasks and people are identified and the timetables established, your next task is to establish regular team meetings. It is imperative that meetings should not be canceled and that there should be 100% attendance. Nothing stops the momentum of team interaction more quickly than one or two canceled meetings. Members immediately start to question your commitment to solving problems. Indeed, a measure of a company's commitment will be whether it will support two hours of involvement per week for each person.

Using the guidelines of the Task Team Process, you are now ready to go through a five-step process which will aid you in the development of an action plan.

ACTION PLAN PROCESS

Plan Development
Execution
Measurement
Evaluation
Corrective Action

This process is similar to the scientific method we were taught early in our careers. You have gathered facts about symptoms and their true, underlying causes. Like a scientist, you devise a hypothesis which attempts to explain why there is a problem and how to eliminate it. This hypothesis is the product of the PLANNING phase. Refer back to the problem solving process in Chapter Six. You then EXECUTE that plan, or test your hypothesis. This can be done via a pilot approach in which you test, measure and then implement. Based on the execution, you gather data on the test and MEASURE what is happening. Then, you EVALUATE your measurements against the plan's original goal. Invariably, there will be some variance between the predicted and the actual results, leading you to take CORRECTIVE ACTION and start the cycle over again. Eventually, you come to a point where your latest analysis correctly identifies the source of the problem and installs a better solution.

When going through the Task Team Process, you will also need to address the making of assignments. We suggest that you find volunteers who have knowledge or expertise in the area under consideration. Often, such a person is the one who suggested the approach or the one who is most adamantly against what is being suggested. Make sure when you assign tasks that you balance the assignments. No person should be allowed to become overburdened.

One more important rule about teams and their administration: The best managed teams are those in which improvement does not end with the completion of the project. This internally developed approach, which is usually aided by the services of outside consultants, creates a greater sense of ownership, acceptance and commitment within the team and throughout the company. It is true that there are basic rules for managing multiple-site companies. Nevertheless, there are differences in culture, attitude and company history. This will make an internally developed program far more effective since the form of process matches the content of the company.

TOOLS FOR A LEADER/FACILITATOR
— The Art of Listening

Working in teams will mean that people must learn to listen. Most of us only remember half of what we hear. Why is this so? What are the barriers to listening? It is not something that just comes to a person. In most instances, teams of people will need to be taught techniques to overcome the barriers to listening. That training begins with learning how to identify these barriers. The following is a list of some of the things which block good listening:

- **Preoccupation with something else.**
  It is difficult to listen to someone else when something is on your mind — e.g., mortgage payments, kids' education, deadlines, etc. You cannot concentrate on what the other person is saying.

- **A mind that is already made up.**
  You cannot listen to someone else when you have a "closed mind" on the subject. As soon as the other person starts to talk, you disagree. Then you either tune the person out or begin planning counter arguments. You are not concentrating on what the other person is saying.

- **Interruptions and distractions.**
  It is almost impossible to listen to someone
  when you are constantly interrupted by
  phone calls, people walking into your office
  or a radio or television playing.

- **Mind wanders (daydreaming).**
  The mind can process information a lot
  faster than people can speak. Unless you
  concentrate on what the speaker is saying,
  your mind begins to use the extra time to
  think about other things.

- **Lack of interest.**
  This is related to daydreaming. When you
  are not personally interested in a topic, it is
  much easier to tune the person out and
  begin thinking about something else.

- **Defensive reaction to criticism.**
  It is difficult to listen to criticism. The
  natural response is to get angry or become
  defensive. You begin thinking about how
  wrong the person is and how you are going
  to rebut his criticism. This response prevents you from listening well enough to
  seriously consider the merit of what the
  person is saying.

As you can probably gather, listening is hard work. In fact,
listening to us means "working to understand." We call this type
of listening, active listening because you are actively involved in
an effort to help the speaker express his or her thoughts and

feelings. To be an active listener requires that you be able to "bracket." Bracketing means being able to set aside your own thoughts and beliefs while you listen to the speaker's side. Active listening also means paraphrasing what the speaker said to make sure that you both agree on what has been said. As such, active listeners usually engage in discussions which involve a slower conversational pace and some periods of silence for reflection.

The techniques below are all proven ways to become a more active listener and to overcome listening barriers:

- **Become active.**
  One of the best ways to combat preoccupation, daydreaming and lack of interest in a topic is to get involved in the discussion. One way to do this is to ask questions, seek clarification, reflect feelings and otherwise become interested.

- **Use "alert" body language.**
  Do not assume a relaxed body posture. Communicate that you are paying attention by an erect posture, by maintaining eye contact and, if seated, by leaning slightly toward the speaker.

- **Remove distractions.**
  If the conversation is important, disconnect the phone or have your calls screened. Close the door to the meeting room or find a quiet place with some privacy. Turn off any radios, televisions or speakers so the speaker can have full attention.

People Empowerment

- **Periodically summarize.**
  One way to keep involved is to periodically
  summarize. This technique works in three
  ways: (1) It forces you to pay attention; (2)
  It indicates to the speaker that you are
  listening well if you summarize correctly;
  and (3) It allows the speaker to correct you
  if are not summarizing correctly which will
  only improve your listening skills more.

- **Acknowledge criticism but don't react.**
  Instead of getting angry or defensive, we
  recommend that you "absorb" the criticism.
  That means acknowledging that the person
  speaking is angry, but not reacting emotionally to that anger. If you don't react, then
  you aren't thinking of excuses, denials or
  rebuttals. Instead, you are listening to what
  the speaker is saying.

TEAM BEHAVIOR GUIDELINES

Criticism can be used as a way to influence someone to change,
but it must be constructive. When it is not constructive, people
become defensive, angry or withdrawn. There are two approaches
to criticism that avoid these negative feelings. One is called the
"Problem Solving" Approach and the other is called the "Direct
Selling" Approach. You can often achieve better results in influ-
encing someone to change by getting them involved through
problem solving. By using this approach, you "depersonalize"
criticism by focusing on a problem, rather than a personality.
There is also an emphasis on listening in this approach.

In the first phase of the "Problem Solving" Approach, you **state the performance discrepancy**. Simply point out the difference between what was expected and what has happened. As noted earlier, you do not criticize, belittle someone's personality, lecture, or beat around the bush.

This done, **ask the team what they think the problem is**. Do not assume that a person was "goofing off." Give the impression that the team is interested only in solving the problem.

The next step is to **listen**. Don't interrupt or argue. Demonstrate that you are genuinely interested in hearing what the person has to say.

Now the problem solving begins. Start this phase by **getting the team members involved**. This starts by asking for their ideas. If the team members don't come up with any ideas, then ask a question related to the problem — who, what, when, where or why?

At J.I. CASE, a team member recently asked the question "why?" and a whole operation was eliminated. The team was looking at a five-step process which took a piece of raw stock and machined it into an axle with a slotted end. One of the steps was a hardening operation in which the slotted end was put into an induction heater. Afterwards, the product was taken out and put on a "straightening" machine. There were a lot of problems at this operation, so the team was looking into buying a new machine. And then, somebody asked why the axle needed to be straightened. It turned out that it needed straightening because the induction heater would warp the axle. If that was the case, said this team member, then maybe we should look at what is wrong with the heater.

The team went and talked with the manufacturer of the heater and found out that current technology would eliminate distortion of the product. The team then realized that the way to eliminate straightening problems was to eliminate the operation by purchasing a new heater. Incidentally, the new heater had a higher price than a new "straightening" machine, but the total cost was much lower since the new heater eliminated a number of quality problems.

Last of all, you must **come to an agreement** on the steps we will take to solve the problem. Make sure that the steps are understood and that everyone has set clear and specific goals.

The purpose of the **"Direct Selling" Approach** is to make criticism a positive instead of a negative experience. You become a salesperson, in effect, who uses persuasion and understanding to show the person the positive aspects of change. The following points are essential to the success of this approach:

- **Be specific.**
  State exactly what it is that you want to change. Don't say that you want "a better attitude" or "better quality." Say you want to cut the set-up time on a certain machine in half or that you must improve quality to 99% by using Statistical Process Control.

- **Concentrate on only one or two changes.**
  The fewer the number of things on which a person has to concentrate, the better he or she will do the job of responding. Select the one or two most important parts of a problem and deal with them first.

- **Show understanding.**
  This is the ability to put yourself in the
  place of the person receiving the criticism.
  What does this person feel and think? It is
  imperative that you let the person know that
  you understand and empathize. Understanding can do much to deaden the sting of
  criticism.

BE POSITIVE, INSTEAD OF NEGATIVE

- **Sell the idea.**
  If you point out the positive aspects of changing in response to criticism, instead of the negative ones, you will find that person responds much more effectively. The result is that they adopt the desired behavior much more quickly.

- **Be brief.**
  The longer you take to point out a problem and explain what you want, the less effective you are in gaining the desired result. There is no reason a criticism session should last longer than three to five minutes. Coaches who scream at team members have less successful results than coaches who give constructive advice as shown in the cartoon on the previous page.

GIVING PRAISE

Although it may not seem as obvious as giving criticism, how you give praise also needs some behavioral guidelines. There are ways of handing out good words that are more effective than others. Here are some of the guidelines we have found most important in our work:

- **Be specific.**
  Like criticism, praise should state exactly what behavior is being rewarded. General praise is bad for two reasons. It doesn't specify what needs to be reinforced and it often comes across as insincere.

- **Be genuine.**
  Make the praise be your personal comment,
  not the comment of the company as a
  whole. Let the person know that you notice
  and appreciate what he or she has done.

- **Be immediate.**
  Give praise as soon after the desired behavior as possible. An informal thank you in
  the hallway five minutes later is more
  effective than a formal handshake two
  weeks later.

- **Don't mix praise with criticism.**
  Doing this gives the person a mixed message and dilutes the power of both messages. If you mix the two, the person only
  waits for the bad news.

- **Don't overuse praise.**
  Overused praise loses its value and effectiveness.

ADMINISTERING MEETINGS

We have all attended meetings that either never really got started
or got going about five minutes before they ended. We have found
that the most effective way to get a meeting started is to ask
leading questions. Try to ask questions which have no right or
wrong answers, but which either seek information or an opinion.
Also make sure that the question only asks for one answer and isn't
so convoluted that people can't understand it. Here are some
examples of the types of questions we mean:

- **Does anyone have a problem with this?**

- **Let's discuss the problem in applying this to your job.**

- **What's the one thing you have learned from this that you can use to do things differently tomorrow?**

The following are suggestions for running a successful meeting:

- **Initiate an agenda prior to the meeting.**

- **Follow the agenda. (see model agenda on next page)**

- **Have all participate by using brainstorming techniques.**

- **Keep focused on the team's objective.**

- **Make assignments.**

- **Summarize meeting activities.**

MODEL AGENDA

_____ **Team**   _____

                              (Date Issued)

_____

(Date and Time of Meeting)

To: _____

_____   **(List All Team**

_____   **Members)**

_____

_____

_____

1. **Review Measurements/Accomplishments.**

2. **List all agenda items carried over from last meeting.**

3. **List all assignments made at the last meeting.**

4. **Review Cause and Effect Diagram (fishbone).**

5. **Discuss and assign action on issues (this removes the constraints to achievement).**

Once a group discussion has started, there are more guidelines for keeping it going. We have found the following to be particularly noteworthy:

> • **Don't allow time-consuming and fruitless arguments.**
> • **Ask people to share experiences and ideas.**
> • **Don't let one or two people dominate.**
> • **Look for opportunities to create action items from discussions.**

The following items should be expected of team members:

> • **Be present at all meetings.**
> • **Be on time.**
> • **Have messages taken and held until after the meeting is over.**
> • **Never walk out of a meeting.**
> • **Be there mentally.**
> • **Remember that it is a <u>team</u> approach.**
> • **All members are equal.**
> • **Be helpful to other members.**
> • **Keep the leader informed.**

Finally, team members have the following responsibilities:

> • **Follow the agenda.**
> • **Participate by doing assignments.**
> • **Plan time for assignments and inform supervisor.**
> • **Follow the problem solving technique.**
> • **Support the decision making process.**
> • **Work toward consensus.**

TEAM PRESENTATIONS

Every team meeting will involve some type of presentation. The purposes of presenting information are to provide communication to the steering committee, to build the confidence of team members and to gain support. Presentations should typically last about 15 to 20 minutes and should be accompanied by an agenda and hand-outs which visually depict what is being discussed. Team presentations should be prepared in advance by gathering quantitative data and by assigning information gathering or measurements tasks to team members. We recommend that team members get together before a presentation in order to determine who will speak on what topic and when and to rehearse what they are going to do and say.

Here is a recommended outline which we have found to be useful for presentations:

TEAM PRESENTATION OUTLINE

I. OPENING
    A. Project's mission or purpose.
    B. Major achievements and/or findings.
    C. Recommended actions for the future.

II. EXPLANATION AND DESCRIPTION
    A. Initial conditions in area of improvement.
    B. Steps taken to eliminate problem; emphasize purpose over step-by-step description.
    C. Results of improvement process.
    D. Demonstration of total cost savings.

III. CLOSING
   A. Summary of the impact of improvement
      process.
   B. Suggestions for continuous improvement in
      future.
   C. Thank-you's to those involved in project.

Refer to Appendix B for sample team presentations.

GENERAL OBSERVATIONS

In concluding this chapter, we leave you with six simple rules which will carry you through every situation and interaction in the team building process. The six rules of behavior for *everybody* in the company are:

> **Be prepared.**
> **Keep focused.**
> **Listen.**
> **Observe.**
> **Be aware of time.**
> **Be respectful.**

Before we move on to the next chapter in which we discuss measurements, here are some more typical questions which arise in a people involvement/empowerment program.

COMMON QUESTIONS AND PROBLEMS

We now come to questions and problems which arise from the implementation of teams. The following questions are actual queries which surfaced at a meeting of a Communication Team in a client's factory.

1. How do you treat all employees equally when they have different levels of knowledge, reading ability, math and writing skills?

Consider remedial education as part of the training and education process. If you think remedial education is expensive, try ignorance! Also, don't patronize less skilled workers by "passing" someone who doesn't make the grade. Don't fire them either — the word will spread. Don't pretend that everyone is equal; the employees know it isn't true and they will not trust you in other areas if you pretend otherwise. Face the issue of different abilities squarely in the face. You will gain much respect if you do.

2. How can we make our communication more effective?

The simple answer is to do everything we suggested in this chapter and to be honest and open. Other suggestions are to publish an in-house newsletter. The key here is visibility. Performance charts indicating progress could be placed on walls. In other words, a little publicity. Communication does not come quickly and, like advertising, the best way to get results is through word-of-mouth. If you are moving in the right direction and make sure everybody knows you are, people will come to you and to each other.

3. How do you get everyone at a team meeting to talk and participate?

Make sure that you have trained your employees in the group facilitation process and that the team is not led by someone who dominates or stifles creativity. Other suggestions are to make sure that the team is talking about a subject they are interested in and that they chose instead of having it forced upon them. Also, improve the team's problem solving skills. Perhaps the problem is too large. Break a problem down into more manageable parts. Brainstorm. Take a break. Create sub-cells to address part of the problem.

If you still have a problem with participation, then address it directly. Sometimes, lack of participation is a passive/aggressive behavior. In other words, workers get back at the company by not doing anything to help. Find out what is behind this behavior. Perhaps a lack of trust in the company? Resentment over past policies? Air out those problems first. If you do, you start to show your trustworthiness and subsequently build a support network.

4. What should we do if a problem starts to come to a head and then we either run out of time or there is a lack of priority?

Define your goals and timetables precisely and realistically. Don't expend 80% of your effort and time on the first 20% of your task. If this is a problem because of a lack of top management commitment, address the problem directly with the team and management. For example, you may need more education in JIT principles to convince people that this work is important.

5. Can problems that have been solved be brought up for discussion again?

The teams will need to know that the decisions made by the group do not have to be permanent. Realizing that it's acceptable to test a solution, the group will feel less reluctant in agreeing on a solution. However, it is equally important that a solution receives a fair trial. There must be an implementation process in place that allows time and the means for evaluating each solution. Unless such a procedure is in place, some issues may never leave the table.

6. What kind of award/reward system should we use and how?

We recommend that you ask your employees what they want as a realistic reward. Management often finds this topic difficult because it is hard to know what satisfies everybody. All the more reason, then, to involve the team in the process of selecting a reward system. For employees, awards/rewards may come as dinners, trips, money, recognition or some combination of all. For suppliers, it might be improved payment terms or cash for on-time delivery. Remember: If you give a little, you may get a lot.

7. How will the group's progress be measured and communicated?

There must be an established methodology for reporting progress. Whatever process you choose, it must be visible to all. What is also important is to adhere to a plan for regularly scheduled communications. This keeps all the people informed of the group's activities and tells the group that what they are doing is important and worthy. This praise will extend to the rest of the people in your company as well.

For information on measuring a team's progress, we now turn to the next chapter.

Chapter Eight

ENSURING
SUCCESS
IN
MEASUREMENT

ENSURING
SUCCESS
IN
MEASUREMENT

MEASURING SUCCESS

The purpose of people involvement/empowerment teams is to seek continuous improvement and the key to improvement is measuring progress from a baseline. Many experts, in fact, believe that most programs fail because the company did not measure performance or did so in a shoddy or incomplete manner. We agree wholeheartedly with this assessment. We have always counseled companies in the importance of measurement. The old axiom below still holds very true:

> ## "That which is measured tends to get better."

First of all, measurements are evidence of progress. No one can argue effectively with numbers that reflect steady improvement.

Second, measurements are important because they are part of a feedback loop which motivates teams to seek even more improvement. To be useful, performance measurements need to be visible for everyone to see. We advocate a Fish Bowl approach, that is, measurements must be displayed in an area that everyone can see so that they know changes for the better are taking place. This approach not only motivates others to get on the PI/E bandwagon, but keeps enthusiasm going for the current teams.

"In God we trust, all others must bring data."

Third, measurements allow companies to judge effectively and quickly whether resources are being allocated to the proper areas in the proper amounts. Fourth, measurements are a means of communicating successes to upper levels of management in order to get and maintain their support for the program. Fifth, as teams eliminate root causes, measurements show improvement and thus validate that the team has solved the problem. Sixth, on-going measurements will indicate whether the problem has reoccurred.

Measurements will become a communication tool which drives the improvement effort through all levels of an organization. Some have even called measurement the lifeblood of the people involvement/empowerment process. The measurements of success should also be communicated to customers and prospects. A company that is moving ahead will be looked upon far more favorably than one which accepts the status quo. Like the illustration on the opposite page demonstrates, measurements or data must be used to convince others of the effectiveness and progress made in the people involvement/empowerment process.

One of our clients, ShareBase (a division of Teradata) publishes a four-page internal newsletter which communicates information about the progress of various teams in the company. The table of contents of a recent issue gives some idea of the range which the newsletter covers:

In this issue:

Corporate	Page 1
Facilities	Pages 1 - 2
Product Integration	Page 2
Marketing	Page 2
Manufacturing	Page 3
Personnel	Pages 3 - 4

The items on these two pages are brief and informal, but informative. Such a communication device does not need to go into great detail. Consider these examples from the newsletter as a guideline for any communication you will undertake:

B² Club '91

The B² Club refers to the "Best of the Best" employees who exemplify Teradata's values and who are consistently high performers. Your coworkers may nominate you as someone who fits the criteria for being the "best of the best." Those selected to be in the B² Club, and a guest, will join approximately 100 other employees to journey to an offsite location in order to attend a team-building conference. This year the site will be the Mauna Lani Hotel on the big island of Hawaii.

MRP II Progress

We are currently on schedule with the installation of our new MRP II software system, with conversion slated for July 1. At this point the pilot phase of the project is being performed to test the functionality and full integration of the package. At the same time, several open issues remain to be resolved prior to the conversion to the new MRP II system.

According to Russ Van Kampen, "A significant amount of time and hard work by several employees has been expended in maintaining this aggressive and optimistic schedule. Our thanks to all for their efforts, cooperation and support."

Quality Teams Save Money

In conjunction with the MRP II system, three
manufacturing quality teams were established.
These teams are comprised of volunteers and
their charter is to find ways to reduce costs and
improve quality. The teams make presentations
to upper management on progress accomplished. Attached are the improvements that the
WOW (War On Waste) team has made to date,
which was recently presented to upper management.

(For more samples of team presentations, see Appendix B.)

Martin Marietta Systems in Orlando, FL also attributes its recent
recognition as a member of the US Army's Contractor Performance Certification Group to the work done by people involve-
ment/empowerment teams who were trained in measuring performance. Martin Marietta calls these groups, Performance Measurement Teams (PMT). They emphasize two key factors in their
success — 1) work center measurements that are accurate and up-
to-date and 2) the allotting of authority to each team to solve
problems. Each PMT at the plant measures the same data in
standards vs. actuals. Some of the data which is collected reflects
first time yields, scrap, lost time, audit and quality reviews,
delivery schedules and so on. Furthermore, all the data is updated
weekly.

These measurements and the performance of the PMT as a group
are evaluated at team meetings. Performance charts play a large
role in graphically showing the amount of progress being made.
Martin Marietta's program has not only notched up significant

numbers — a 13% improvement in yield, 81.4% reduction in manufacturing rework, a 61% decrease in overtime — but it has caught fire with other disciplines within the company. Now, everybody is talking about jumping on the PMT wagon.

The Baldrige award is another means whereby companies can measure themselves for success. Many people feel that the real importance and benefit of this award is the fact that it fosters knowing how your company is doing. Constant measurement means that a company is making its problems visible so there can be continuous improvement. The Baldrige committee examines the following seven criteria. These are the areas you should consider measuring as well.

BALDRIGE AWARD CRITERIA

- Leadership — The senior management's success in creating and sustaining a quality culture.

- Information and Analysis — The effectiveness of the company's collection and analysis of information for quality improvement and planning.

- Planning — The effectiveness of integration of quality requirements into the company's business plans.

- Human Resource Utilization — The success of the company's efforts to utilize the full potential of the work force for quality.

- Quality Assurance — The effectiveness of the company's systems for assuring quality control of all operations.

- Quality Assurance Results — The company's results in quality achievements and quality improvement, demonstrated through quantitative measures.

- Customer Satisfaction — The effectiveness of the company's systems to determine customer requirements and demonstrated success in meeting them. Finalists are subject to an on-site visit by examiners to verify their quality programs.

TYPES OF MEASUREMENT

People teams will measure several areas. Starting at the top, management commitment is measured to ensure their participation in supporting team activity. Process measurements determine how effectively the people involvement/empowerment program is being managed and administered. For example, many companies keep records of when teams were established, when they started to function and when they disbanded. This is done to see how long it takes to complete a specific task. If the team goes beyond the normal time span, it may be an indication that the team needs more resources or that the original task was too large of an undertaking. By keeping records like this, you will be able to fine tune your own people involvement/empowerment process.

Performance measurements show tangible results of what they have accomplished. There are four main types. They are Quality of Product, Productivity, Service and Quality of Work Life. Besides the obvious benefit of letting a team know how they are progressing, performance measurements also are valuable records for teams to use as a base for improvement. Future teams can learn from the successes of previous teams and build toward more progress. Again, the theme of continuous improvement arises. It is a philosophy that all would-be World Class companies must subscribe to.

EXAMPLES OF PERFORMANCE MEASUREMENTS

The World Class Company's hardest task is to establish meaningful measurements. We must be sure that all measurements are interrelated for the achievement of World Class Status. The key is to establish a baseline today with goals and objectives which must be accomplished. Once a baseline is established, companies measure and monitor their progress toward the goal. Perhaps most importantly measurements are useful as a dynamic management tool which establishes a results orientation in the workplace. Measurement graphs like the ones which follow should be displayed throughout the plant for people to see.

Number of Defects

Purpose: This measurement tracks items which are received with defects from suppliers. You should analyze why and what the effect of this measurement is on your company. Of course, companies should be moving toward a zero-defect policy in which defects are discovered by the processor while manufacturing a product.

Responsibility: The responsibility for this measurement should be with Production and Inventory Control and/or Purchasing. However, the data needs to be provided by Incoming Inspection.

Reporting: The measurements should include graphs which reflect the number, percent and cost of defects. Reports should reflect performance by supplier and the total supply base.

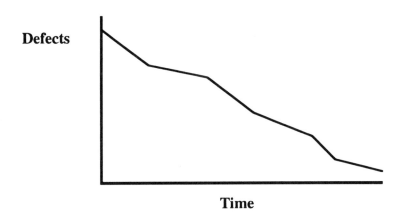

Time

Tracking Costs:

Inspection cost, processing cost, distribution cost.
Inspection cost = Cost of labor to inspect all parts to find bad ones + equipment cost + carrying cost.
Processing cost = Cost of maintaining data and records on defects.
Distribution cost = Labor to move it + packing + shipping.

Incoming Parts Inspected

Purpose: This measurement reflects the ability of a company to work with its suppliers to receive defect-free parts and toward completely eliminating incoming inspection.

Responsibility: Responsibility should be with the Supplier Certification team and Quality function. Every effort should be made to obtain zero-defect parts and eliminate inspection techniques.

Reporting: This measurement should take the form of a graph which represents the percentage of parts still being inspected. Reports can reflect the dollars expended on inspection for individual products and as an aggregate number.

Calculation of dollars: Dollars spent = Labor + material + equipment.

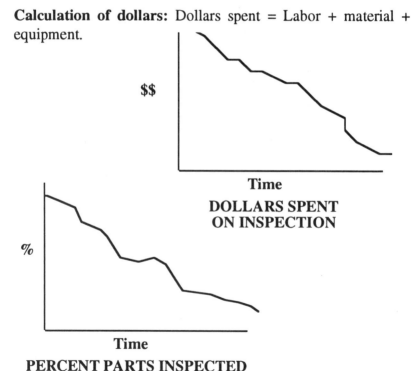

Time
**DOLLARS SPENT
ON INSPECTION**

Time
PERCENT PARTS INSPECTED

Scrap and Rework

Purpose: Both scrap and rework represent waste to World Class efforts. They indicate a company's inability to produce a product right the first time. Measurements allow the company to note improvement in reducing this waste.

Responsibility: To determine responsibility, the company must first determine why scrap and rework is produced. The causes need to be identified, displayed with the use of a Pareto chart and the root causes eliminated by the responsible function.

Reporting: Measurements need to be recorded in both reports and graphs. Graphs make visible the severity of the problem and the amount of dollars lost. Reports reflect the opportunity to reduce cost through the elimination of waste.

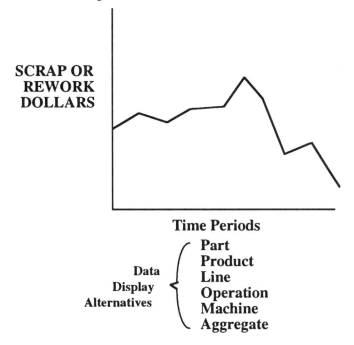

Other Quality Measurements

- Number of Floor Parts Inspected.

- Hours of Inspection.

- Operations under SPC.

- Operators Trained in SPC.

- Training Hours and Dollars per Employee.

- Cost of Quality.

- Material Acquisition Cost.

On-Time Delivery

Purpose: All departments providing service to both internal and external customers should track their ability to deliver to the agreed-upon date. This measurement should be communicated back to the supplier. For example, Order Entry should measure customer delivery.

Responsibility: In most companies , the computer system should provide Purchasing and Order Entry with an on-time delivery measurement. If not, the data should be collected manually by Purchasing and Receiving functions as well as Order Entry and Shipping.

Reporting: This measurement should be made into a graph which reflects the variances to the delivery date. The causes should be analyzed so that internal and external improvements can be made.

EXTERNAL CUSTOMER

Company _____

TABLE

Month	Total Shipped	#/% On-time	Late →			
			1-5	6-10	11-15	16+
Jan.	100	90/90%	2/2%	0/0%	5/5%	3/3%

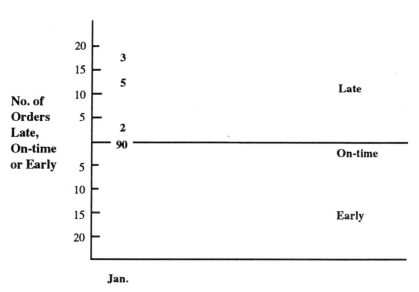

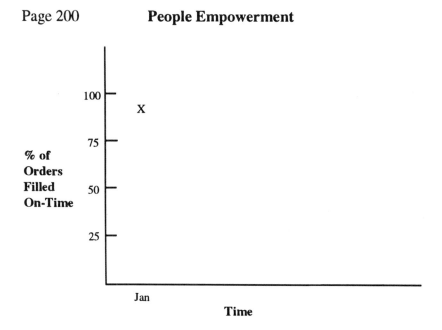

Material Moves

Purpose: The movement of materials through the company is non-productive and therefore waste. Movement in and out of inventory, from one operation to another and from plant to warehouse needs to be identified, analyzed and then eliminated.

Responsibility: Each function that deals with materials should be asking itself how the material arrives and where the next receiving area is. These functions need to take responsibility for finding ways to reduce the effort and the time it takes to move material through the company. This measurement can also apply to non-material moves such as engineering change orders, invoices, production schedules and packing slips.

Reporting: Measurements should be represented on a graph showing the time involved in moving something and subsequent dollars saved.

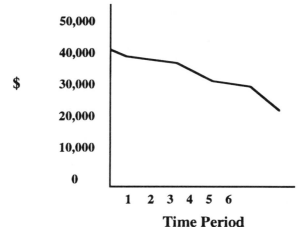

MATERIAL MOVEMENT
DOLLARS SAVED
DEPT XYZ

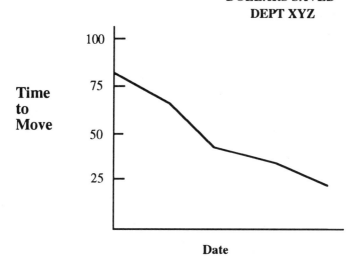

TIME FOR MOVEMENTS

Calculation of Dollars:

Material moves into and out of inventory = Parts x average moves. (Computer transactions should provide number of moves and number of parts.)

9,000 = 3,000 parts x 3 average moves.

Dollars to move = $5. (Represents estimate of labor and equipment usage.)

Total dollars = Parts x average moves x dollars to move.

$45,000 = 3,000 x 3 x $5.

Note: Dollars are not to the bottom line, but are reflected in overhead and should be used to emphasize the need to reduce the number of moves in a World Class operation.

Lead-Time

Purpose: This measurement allows the facility to track conformance to stated lead times. It should reflect the effort made in reducing lead-time, an important goal of World Class manufacturers.

Responsibility: The operations function should be responsible for capturing the necessary data. All areas employing lead-time should be included, such as: Order entry, Purchasing, Shipping functions (including paperwork), In-transit times and Kitting. In addition, lead-time elements can be tracked such as the following: Queue, Set-up, Run (machine and/or labor), Wait and Move.

Reporting: Reports should indicate product performance reductions. A baseline should be established and goals set to be measured against.

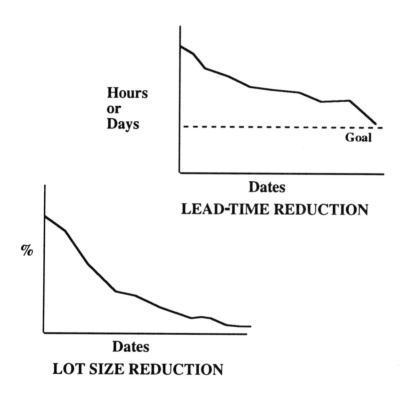

LEAD-TIME REDUCTION

LOT SIZE REDUCTION

Uptime

Purpose: Uptime represents a measurement of productive manufacturing operations. Equipment stoppage can be caused by tools, material, documentation or people. Regardless of the reason, downtime is a waste and must be recognized, monitored and eliminated.

Responsibility: The team's function must be to react as quickly as possible to direct the necessary resources needed to resolve the issue.

Reporting: To obtain the data for this measurement, it is necessary for someone to log the time from work stoppage until the operation is up and running at normal operating efficiency. Reports and graphs should reflect hours and dollars lost. Dollars should show both labor and lost production.

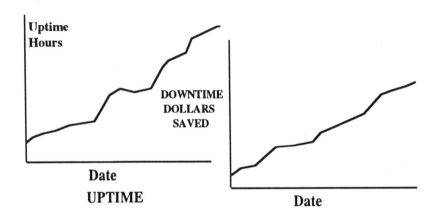

Quantity Variances

Purpose: This measurement places an emphasis on getting the exact quantity of parts requested from suppliers. Variances, plus or minus, are used to analyze their effect on the organization.

Responsibility: Purchasing and/or Internal Production Control should maintain this measurement from data provided by Receiving and Inspection.

Reporting: Reports should reflect either the number short or over and the effects should be captured on a Pareto chart. Separate reports should be produced for each supplier.

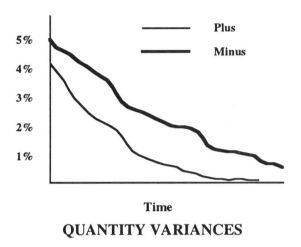

Time

QUANTITY VARIANCES

Set-Up Reduction

Purpose: Set-up reduction measurements show a company's improvement in several ways. We first want to perform set-up in less time. Then, as we reduce the time, we should also reduce the lot size. By reducing lot size, the company can be more flexible in the production mix needed to meet real customer requirements.

Responsibility: Set-up reduction needs to be attacked through the use of teams. Teams are responsible for achieving continuous goals of a 50 percent reduction on a no cost/low cost effort.

Reporting: Measurements for set-up reduction should also be reported in graphs and reports. Graphs reflect minutes and hours reduced, lot size reduction, productivity improvements, inventory reduction and cost savings. Reports should reflect cost reduction and increased unit production.

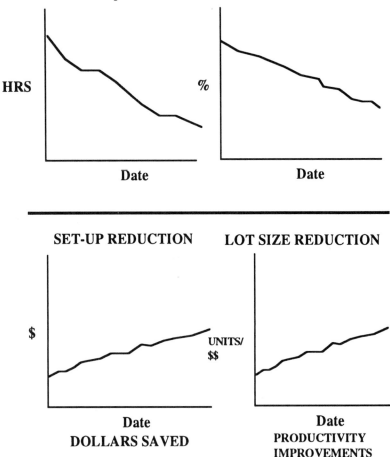

SET-UP REDUCTION   LOT SIZE REDUCTION

DOLLARS SAVED   PRODUCTIVITY IMPROVEMENTS

Cost vs. Benefits

Purpose: This measurement allows management to track the progress of continuous improvement programs. All costs expended for programs are measured against cost savings realized.

Responsibility: Responsibility lies with the teams or project leaders to capture the data from their programs and to summarize totals for management. A goal and/or a period of time should be established for the point at which benefits outweigh costs.

Reporting: This measurement should be in the form of a graph which is manually prepared from data captured by the teams.

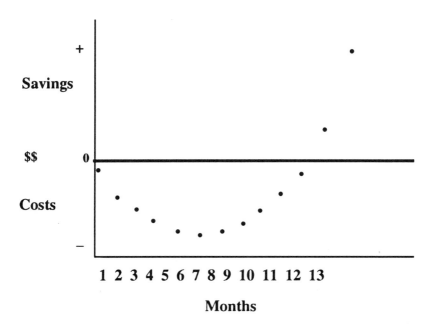

Additional Measures

A good overall measurement of quality management can be obtained by tracking customer service whether inside or outside of the company. For example, look at the number of customer orders filled as scheduled or requested. Also measure the number of customer complaints per product shipped.

Consider including the number of teams formed and types of teams, including what each team accomplished. This would give management a capsule overview.

We did not try to include every possible index, formula or ratio that exists. We did include those key measurements, which if not measured, will result in failure on your journey to World Class.

STRESS, TIME AND ENERGY
— Pulling It All Together

Working on a team does not need to be stressful. On the contrary, the excitement of helping a company succeed in the global marketplace is a very rewarding experience for all involved. There are some guidelines, however, that can make the expenditure of time and energy go more smoothly. We recommend that teamwork should be allotted a predetermined amount of time. A good rule of thumb is to commit the company to providing two hours per week for each employee to participate on a team. Part of the training that every team member should receive is instruction in how to manage meeting time so that the agenda gets accomplished.

As for energy, make sure that great care is taken in assigning tasks correctly. No person should be given too much to accomplish. Spread tasks among team members and devise challenging, but reasonable timeframes.

Lastly, we strongly suggest, strange as it may sound, that people be given the opportunity to fail. More often than not, Thomas Edison's statement about genius is correct. It is 1% inspiration and 99% perspiration. That means you must give team members the time and the resources to find the right answer, not the band-aid approach. Any great project which has blazed a new path has come about because a team of people took the time to do it the right way. Here's to your success on this long and hard, but highly successful, journey on the path of people involvement/empowerment. We hope you have a good time.

Chapter Nine

PRO-TECH
CASE
STUDIES

PRO-TECH
CASE
STUDIES

The following case studies describe activities and results at several of our clients.

ALLIED SIGNAL
BENDIX
FRICTION MATERIALS DIVISION
Troy, New York and Cleveland, Tennessee

This case study demonstrates how a team addresses and devises solutions to various problems as well as showing the great benefits to be accrued from people involvement/empowerment.

Set-up reduction teams can accomplish significant reductions in machine changeover times using simple, practical and inexpensive methodologies. This is exactly what happened when teams were established at our client, the Friction Materials Division of Bendix in Cleveland, TN, and Troy, NY. With Project Engineer

Joe Bedard acting as a facilitator and manager, these teams were able to reduce a particular set-up from 12 hours to 1 hour and 10 minutes. Still another set-up went from 65 minutes to 12 minutes. What is most surprising is that most of these reductions were the result of a "first pass" at the problem. In other words, further reductions are possible.

These results are even more phenomenal when it is realized that as little as $700 was spent in yielding an 80 percent reduction in set-up time on one machine. Other set-up reduction efforts were accomplished well below budget as well.

The team's strategy was to identify those machines which caused production constraints, or bottlenecks, and to attack the set-up time of each. A reduction in set-up time would allow for smaller lot sizes and, most importantly, greater flexibility. Several kinds of brakes could then be produced in order to meet customer demand. In other words, Bendix was looking to build today what it sold yesterday in order to attain 100 percent customer service as the following examples show.

The Briquette Press

The Briquette press is responsible for producing front disc brake pads which are sold to U.S. auto manufacturers and to Toyota. Basically, the machine indexes to various stations where the pad material and the backing material are dispensed and compressed. The finished unit is then sent on to an oven for the final hardening.

The process begins when a hopper dispenses a predetermined amount of backing material on to a conveyor. The conveyor then drops the material into a mold on a turntable. The turntable indexes to the first station where a tamping foot compresses the material. After indexing again, the turntable rotates the compressed material in the mold to the second station where a metallic compound is dropped on top of the backing material. The mold is then indexed to a third station where, like the first station, a tamp foot compresses the metallic compound. At the fourth station, the newly formed briquette is ejected from the mold and goes down a chute where it waits to be brought to the hardening oven.

After receiving training from Mike Gozzo, Joe Bedard and the set-up team used a videotape to observe that there were well over 50 bolts which had to be loosened, removed and then tightened again. Many of these bolts were not very accessible. The tamp foot for the backing material used to be composed of 5 parts. By simplifying the design of this tool, the set-up team was able to reduce the number of parts to one. Furthermore, the team placed two ratcheting handles on the tamp foot. All it takes to release or lock the piece now is a one-half turn.

The bolts holding the tamp foot in place were also replaced with one-third turn fasteners. These fasteners allow the set-up person to remove the tamp foot without disconnecting the entire assembly. Before set-up reduction, the height of the tamp foot was determined by "touch-feel-go" adjusting by the set-up person. The team decided to eliminate adjustment by presetting the height of the tamp foot for each different kind of brake pad. No more adjustment was needed. It should be noted here that the changes which occurred at the tamping station for the backing material were also implemented at the tamping station for the metallic compound. Thus, one solution resolved two problems.

All of these set-up reduction techniques, which cost approximately $700 to implement, resulted in a reduction of over 80 percent in set-up time (from 65 minutes to 12 minutes).

Drills on Wheels

One $18,000 drilling machine at Bendix would have needed
$12,000 in improvements in order to significantly reduce set-up
time. The team could find no way to reduce set-up time using the
"no-cost/low-cost" set-up reduction principles they had been
taught in three days of training. Eventually, the team found a
solution. It was to put the entire drilling machine on locking
casters and to provide quick disconnects for all the air hoses,
electrical conduits and ductwork connected to the machine.

The idea behind these changes was to make it possible to remove
one drilling machine after the job was done and replace it with an
entirely different drilling machine which was set-up for the next
job. In other words, the entire set-up time was virtually eliminated
by making all of it external. When Part #1 was running, Drilling
Machine #2 was set up to run Part #2. When Part #1 was finished,
Drill Machine #1 was disconnected and Drill Machine #2 was
rolled and locked into place. What used to take 35 minutes and was
fraught with quality problems now takes 5 minutes and runs
trouble-free.

There are some that still say this isn't set-up reduction because the
machine still takes the same amount of time to set up and that there
has been no improvement. But, this is an example of true set-up
reduction because there is now increased uptime available on this
machine. In other words, Bendix' capacity problems were solved
and Bendix was provided the flexibility to respond to auto makers
constant schedule changes.

As this case study so vividly shows, people involvement and
empowerment is simple, practical and cost justified. When a
company decides, as Bendix decided, to let loose the creative

power of their people, there is literally no end to the benefits which will accrue. Time and time again, we see people participation as a consistently successful answer to the problems facing companies today.

This case study is taken from **Set-Up Reduction: Saving Dollars with Common Sense,** *Jerry W. Claunch and Philip D. Stang, PT Publications, Palm Beach Gardens, FL, 1989, p. 238-245.*

J.I. CASE
Racine, Wisconsin

This case study demonstrates how a company got the support of the union up front for a people involvement/empowerment program. Doing so made all the difference in the world between acceptance and rejection.

At this particular client, Pro-Tech worked with Andre Cariello, plant manager, and Jim Barbieri, quality assurance manager, in implementing a Total Quality Management program. Mike Gozzo, Phil Stang and Mel Pilachowski (all of Pro-Tech) were brought into this tractor assembly plant employing 1,000 people on multiple shifts to improve a problem in what the company called the "hospital," or repair, area. The plant was building 40 tractors a day, but approximately 25 of them were being rejected. The rejected tractors sat in the hospital until they were repaired.

Our strategy was first to expose direct labor to both TQM and Just-In-Time (JIT) and how the two concepts related to each other in the manufacturing environment. The union, the United Auto

Workers, was initially doubtful. We have found this to be almost universally true and it is because union personnel are rarely involved or asked to participate from the beginning in new programs affecting direct labor. Our goal, then, was to bring the union in from the start so that they, and not us or company management, would provide the empowerment to their people. The plan was to have the union people institute major parts of the program themselves. This indeed was the case. The union played a primary role in getting the program off the ground because they had the authority to make things happen without the need for direct approval by company management.

The company soon faced a crucial test over how strong their commitment was to letting people be empowered. Engineers were selected to become members of all teams in the company's TQM program. On one team which was working on reducing set-up time on an axle cell assembly, there was an engineer who constantly resisted accepting the suggestions of the other team members. This was causing a great deal of frustration on the team. People on the team looked at the situation as some sort of test in which they would see whether or not the company would truly support the wishes of the team members. They wanted management to relieve the engineer of his duties on the team.

The team, in consultation with Pro-Tech consultants, decided first to go one-on-one with the engineer. The team leader sat down with him and attempted to get a more positive attitude and level of participation from the engineer by discussing the problem. This did not work. The team leader then turned to one of the facilitators to address such issues.

The issue now facing this facilitator was this: "How do you replace team members who are negative and oppositional?" To make a long story short, the facilitator went to management and suggested that they allow the team to replace the engineer with somebody the team could select. Management did not stand in the way and allowed the team to act.

Another area where the company's commitment was put to a challenge was in the funding of the entire project. J.I. Case initially funded the program. This included buying videotape equipment for set-up reduction analysis and providing the full administrative support of two full-time facilitators from the direct labor union force. The union directed all of this activity. The company also decided that subsequent funding would come from savings generated by the activities of the teams. A portion of the savings would go to the company and the remaining portion to funding more projects. The teams and facilitators were allowed to decide which education and training programs they needed in order to gain expertise. This was necessary so they could continue the participatory model they had started and thus include more and more people.

The initial education and training program of JIT and TQM as well as team building and problem solving became an on-going activity. For instance, as one team delved deeper and deeper into some problems, they realized that they needed a better understanding of inventory. They requested education and training in that area.

Another team wanted to establish a better mechanism to gain control of recording and obtaining information from work-in-process, shipping and receiving. They requested and received education and training sessions in bar coding. As you can see, it wasn't long before the people in this company were moving faster than management ever expected. Just another example of the power of people involvement/empowerment.

BARR LABORATORIES
Pomona, New York

This high-growth company knew what they wanted: a people involvement/empowerment program to last. They knew that using their most powerful resource — people — was the best way to face the future.

Barr Labs, as noted in Chapter Four, is a pharmaceutical manufacturer of generic controlled drugs which it sells to major drugstore chains. The key players, as we have shown, were Gerry Price, executive vice president, and union leader Judy Contreras.

Pro-Tech first started working with Barr Labs at the request of Gerry who brought us in to teach the concept of Just-In-Time/ Total Quality Control (JIT/TQC). Gerry's intention was to institute change in the company so that it could become a World Class manufacturer, but change which would be kept under control in an environment of rapid growth.

It was a tall order. As you know, a company in a growth mode encounters many problems which threaten the company's ability to keep its niche and to satisfy market needs. With rapid growth, many companies lose control of the way they do business. Costs skyrocket and waste of all types explodes. Gerry asked us to help him maintain control while expanding the company through increased profits and increased volume. He reasoned, and we agreed, that a program of continuous improvement was essential and the only way to insure the success of such a program was to involve and empower the people who worked at Barr Labs.

As always, education and training were at the core of our activities. The reason is simple. If you are going to ask people to take responsibility for their own destiny, then they need tools in order to execute the plans they devise. As mentioned in Chapter Four, everybody agreed that education and training had to be provided on a continuous basis in order to get the desired results instead of relying on "education by injection," or a one-shot panacea.

One way this was accomplished was to expose new people who were hired to the continuous improvement attitude. Such an introduction included the basic skills needed to make the whole program work, such as Total Quality Management, Just-In-Time, Statistical Process Control (SPC), Set-up Reduction, Problem solving and Team building. This introduction was given roughly every quarter to 30-35 people who had been hired in the previous three months. The overall philosophy session which kicked off the introduction lasted a full day.

The results were almost immediate. There was a tangible decrease in fear about losing jobs and a tangible increase in confidence as people began to realize that they were expected to attempt solutions as part of a team without going through a cumbersome and slow process of management approval. One of our directors, Tom Petroski, reported that a lab person had used SPC to prove the viability of a new tracking device which tested chemicals being received. This one development alone resulted in an annual savings of $100,000. People involvement/empowerment really does pay off!

LORAN
A Division of the LORANGER CORP.
Warren, Pennsylvania

Once upper management bought into the concept of a people

involvement/empowerment program, Loran was able to field teams capable of solving problems and pull the division out of a prolonged slump.

As noted earlier in the book, Loran is a family-owned manufacturer of audio cassettes for major automotive manufacturers and for the music industry. Rob Loranger, the president of the division, learned about the human orientation of business while attending Harvard University. He felt that his division had to show leadership in the people area, but he didn't quite know the pragmatic side of how to begin. Pro-Tech came in at this point.

The existing condition of the division at that time was that it was flirting between breaking even and not being profitable. Rob Loranger felt that they needed something beyond what he had just learned at a Dr. Deming seminar about how management should serve the worker, instead of the other way around. Given this situation, the primary thrust of our intervention was first to get support and buy-in from all of the upper management staff.

Initially, there was some resistance and we needed to provide some individualized, one-on-one education and training for some of the staff. Rob also shifted some of his key personnel from one position to another in order to get the right talent combination. In addition to these activities, we also put on a series of education courses which started with team play, team building, behavioral understanding of group dynamics as well as courses designed to be used as tools: resolving behavioral problems, time management and problem solving.

Once this was accomplished, we then turned to the work force of 75 people and began the process of having them buy in to the program. It has been our experience over the years in all types and sizes of companies that the people's buy-in will be easier and quicker if management demonstrates its willingness to trust the teams and grant them true authority and responsibility. One of the team members wrote the following testimonial about that process in a team report:

> ## "When I started, I was a skeptic. I became a participant. As a result of that, I am now an advocate."
> *Rich Zydonik*

Rich made this statement as a result of some work being done by his team on a problem in the production of a component known as an idler arm. Quality Assurance had informed the team that it was at the top limits of the specifications for a critical dimension (the height of a seat). If the problem was not resolved, the tape in the cassette would not be able to move freely, obviously a problem requiring immediate attention.

The molding department tried several times to adjust the process in order to bring the part back into acceptable limits, but weren't successful. We then moved into a brainstorming session. One person in Quality Assurance noted that in the previous run, the parts were below the top limits. This data was brought up on the computer and confirmed. Somebody from the machine shop then said that the problem appeared when the molding was being done at a supplier. He thought that the molders might have put a shim in front of the ejector rod to make the part smaller. While we never dismiss any ideas in a brainstorming session, none of the team members thought this was a possibility.

At the same time as this was happening, one of the members of the molding maintenance team went to the computer and pulled down some data showing the date of the size change in the parts. He then retrieved the downtime reports for the same period of time. These reports showed that another shift indicated downtime for a threaded ejector rod which had broken. The rod was replaced at the time and the press restarted. Nobody thought that a 1/4-turn on a nut could make a change in dimensions, but since we were looking for only a thousandth of an inch, we decided to test our theory. Sure enough, it was the answer. The team made the necessary adjustments and the press produced parts well within the specification limits.

This is what Rich Zydonik had to say about the team's actions:

> **"Team effort works. Data collection is necessary. Our downtime tracking along with the new computer in the department are big tools in this process. Tight tolerances in molding can be affected by seemingly unrelated causes. This experience again proves that Loran is doing the utmost and that the people are doing their best to maintain the high standards of the products being produced."**
>
> *Rich Zydonik*

It was abundantly clear in dealing with Loran that they were successful because they were able to maintain focus by paying attention to these areas:

- **Patience.**
- **Research.**
- **Accumulation of data.**
- **Continuous measurement of performance.**

And, of course, to use the knowledge, intelligence and experience of people in brainstorming in trying to determine causes and then solving the problem at hand.

Shortly after this occurred, Loran had to make a presentation to a new customer (3M). Loran was able to show with facts, figures and graphs what they had accomplished, not with just words. For instance, Loran's profit and loss statement in September 1990 showed it to be 4 percent of sales. By June 1991 (four measured quarters later), the percent of sales had jumped to 10 percent. This was the same time period when downtime on equipment started being measured as well as associated costs and the number of defects.

Productivity had risen even though sales remained relatively flat. Volume of output was greater with the same number of hours being expended. In August 1990, the pieces per machine hour for a base and cover assembly was at 1,200 units, its lowest point. By May 1991, that figure had risen to 1,600 units. In a related operation downstream, the pieces per machine hour was 1,045 units in August 1990. By May 1991, it had risen to 1,180 units.

That was a greater than 10 percent increase, all because people were now monitoring the process. Think how such figures could impress your customers. People involvement/empowerment works toward the bottom line.

SHAREBASE
A Division of the TERADATA CORP.
Los Gatos, California

A people involvement/empowerment program was used at this computer manufacturer to achieve results in a shorter time frame. All involved learned that there is power in people organized as a team and who are directly impacting their own destinies.

ShareBase is a high-end computer manufacturer (one level below a Cray) whose customers include AT&T, NASA, Department of Defense and K-Mart. Approximately 200 people work at this site, 150 in engineering support and 50 in direct labor. The principal management people involved in the program were Michael Reiff, President, Mark Cosmez, Chief Financial Officer, and Peter Garcia, Materials Director.

The objectives of the program were: 1) to select and implement new computer software which would be used to run the business; 2) to make the people involvement/empowerment part of the mental processes of people both in the support operations and in the direct labor force; and 3) to drive forth a statement on quality and the reduction of costs associated with quality as well as to obtain a subsequent throughput increase over the same time period.

Work of this nature is typically done in a year, but we established an eight-month timeframe. Within this timeframe, the company fielded four teams — Internal Quality, External Quality, Internal Flow, and a Module Team (responsible for selection and implementation of a new computer system). The results were more than gratifying. The new computer system was put into physical operation in six months. That set a record for both ShareBase and for us at Pro-Tech. The other teams also reported significant savings.

External Quality, for instance, worked on a PC board connector problem by sitting down with the supplier and inside technical support staff and resolved a situation which had plagued them for the past two years. Internal Quality worked on a problem on the assembly line concerning cabling. This team with the assistance of operators on the floor made a change in the process of checking for continuity of the cable inside the computer. This change eliminated 25 percent of the handling time associated with moving parts between assembly areas.

Internal Quality also worked on a SCSI cable connector inside the computer. Its variable length was causing some problems with customers, the sales department reported. The team, after interfacing with sales, engineering and operators, decided that the question of length was best left for the operators to decide. This minimized the efforts of Material Engineering spending several hours trying to ascertain what length of cable the customer required.

Meanwhile, the Internal Flow team worked in two areas. The first area involved the computer's power supply board. After each of these units was received from the supplier, ShareBase did 30 hours of burn-in time on each and every one. One operator couldn't understand why this was done because the failure rate was practically nil. He also noted that ShareBase did another burn-in to integrate the whole system. He thought the initial burn-in was redundant. After checking Receiving's burn-in results, the team decided to contact the supplier. It turned out that the supplier was already doing the burn-in before it left their plant. Based on that information, the team decided to eliminate the burn-in for these boards. Needless to say, there was an appreciable direct savings which was realized immediately.

Internal Flow also established a new flow for the entire operation. As the charts on the next two pages show, there was much wasted activity and crisscrossing in the "before" flow. The current floor layout is much less complicated.

All of the above efforts were executed primarily because owner-ship was given to all the people involved, from the simplest activity on the floor to the selection and implementation of a brand-new computer system. Supervisors like Art Ordonio and Joe Casteel were team members, not leaders. Providing people the opportunity to participate and giving them the authority to make decisions is what makes change happen. This philosophy was initially opposed by some members of ShareBase's management.

For example, ShareBase's Chief Financial Officer had never seen the structure, organization and techniques we employed at work before. He was used to getting a computer system selected and implemented by using more traditional practices. In this old system, the work is done primarily by a program manager who directs everything. It is a top-down approach in which decisions are pushed onto people rather than having people decide what they need and then request from management the resources to make it happen. This is what we helped start at ShareBase — a process

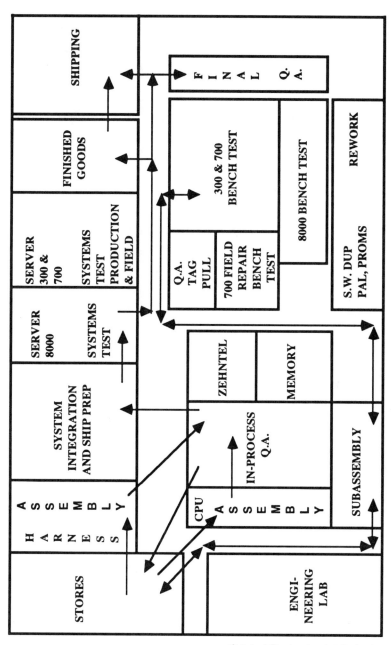

Original Design by Art Ordonio

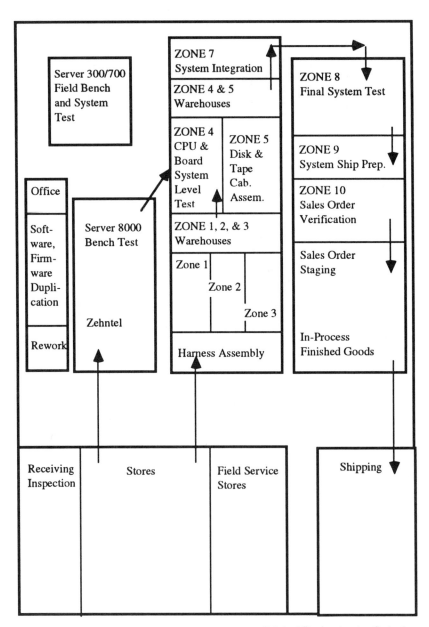

Original Design by Art Ordonio

whereby respective module leaders were responsible for their area from the beginning to the end of the project. The result, as mentioned before, was so impressive that Mark Cosmez completely reversed his view. He informed us that if he ever had to do it again, he would use our methodology of people involvement/ empowerment.

APPLE COMPUTER
Freemont, California

A people involvement/empowerment program has been part of Apple's philosophy for a long time. The following is a summary of the methods employed by Pro-Tech co-founder, president and chief executive officer Peter L. Grieco, Jr. as director of operations at the Macintosh facility.

First of all, we recognized that we needed a vision of what the department could accomplish. If it wasn't clear to us, if it wasn't more than a mirage, then there was no way for me to get the excitement across to the people who worked with me. That capacity to communicate the vision in order to gain support or buy-in was the second activity I undertook. All the talk in the world, of course, is useless if you are not going to let people own their part of the whole. I had seen too many managers and supervisors who let their egos get in the way of doing the job right. A manager is not judged on how many good ideas he or she has or even on how well the ideas are communicated. We are judged on results and that means we need the cooperation and the enthusiasm of people who work with us.

Success, then, is based on how well a manager allows the people in a department to assume responsibility and exercise authority. In a way, the success of a World Class manager is how well he or she relinquishes control to others.

While at Apple, we followed many of the ideas presented in the pages in this book. I tried to become an effective leader by recognizing the importance of people as innovators and individuals. I saw one of my primary functions as being a team developer. This meant that I needed to let people know that I trusted them and that they could fail, if they could learn from their mistakes. Somebody once said that almost every important invention was accomplished by the wrong person at the wrong time and for the wrong reason. When people have the courage to go against the grain and ask "Why?" every time they hear the same old explanation, that's when we will have progress.

Anybody who has met me knows that "Why?" is my favorite word. Some people think I ask that question just to be a pain and that I don't care what they have to say. Nothing could be further from the truth. I'm waiting for somebody to give me an answer, an answer that leaves me satisfied. When I see somebody hemming and hawing, I know that they haven't thought out the problem. If they had, they could tell me why I should accept what they say.

I believe that the use of teams is the best way to come up with answers to the question "Why?" That's because a good team is composed of members trained in problem solving techniques. In essence, they have already learned how to ask "Why?" several times. I strongly believe that people will do their work more efficiently and intelligently if management lets them use their brains to their fullest capacities.

CARDOLITE CORPORATION
Newark, New Jersey

*Pro-Tech was asked to initiate a people involvement/empower-
ment program at this company in order to help it increase
productivity. Even companies which are prospering need to look
toward the future.*

Cardolite Corporation is a manufacturer of specialty chemicals
for various industries, including the automotive industry. This
privately-held company, which employs approximately 70 people,
came to us with some problems that many companies wished they
had. Cardolite was faced with numerous opportunities to sell
current products within their present markets and to new markets.
They also had the opportunity to sell newly developed products to
present and new markets. Unfortunately, the company was not in
a position to exploit these opportunities to their fullest. Cardolite
was concerned about whether it could produce enough of its
product to meet these demands.

The principal issue, since they already manufactured a quality
product, was how Production was going to meet the demand. Over
the course of several years, President Tony Stonis had found that
productivity had been slipping while costs were increasing. During those years, he had attempted to rectify the problem by talking
with his managers and supervisors. These talks were, at various
times, either cheerleading or coaxing sessions designed to get
them to increase production and reduce costs. Stonis was frustrated in his efforts, however, until he attended one of Pro-Tech's
supplier symposia at Bendix Brake Division.

Our talk about Total Quality Management, Supplier Certification and the Continuous Improvement Process covered the topics which Stonis was looking to implement at his company. Stonis was also looking for something other than a top-down, autocratic approach. In fact, in our discussions, he expressed his frustration that this approach made him the least powerful individual in the company to effect change.

We began our work at Cardolite in May with an assessment. From this initial activity, we decided to implement two teams of eight people each. The teams would include supervision and hourly workers. One team addressed housekeeping around the plant while the other team addressed waste minimization.

On the housekeeping team, we encountered a person who not only had doubts about whether people involvement/empowerment would work, but was very reluctant about being team leader. It turned out that Dominick Dacunha, like many people who become involved in a people involvement/empowerment program, did not have the skill set necessary to facilitate team meetings. We worked with him over the next several months to bring him up to speed. This was accomplished by gradually allowing Dominick to assume more and more responsibilities at each meeting while we continued to be the principal facilitator. At the first meeting in which he was team leader, he introduced the agenda for the day in order to get used to talking in front of a group. After five or so meetings, he started to become more involved as we backed off in coordinating the meetings. We would talk to him quietly during a meeting whenever he needed help in addressing some of the issues, such as how to get a reluctant individual to participate.

A year later, Dominick is very enthused about the team process and doesn't think they could have accomplished what they did without people involvement/empowerment. He has become a highly skilled team leader and is adept at drawing people out and building a consensus.

This same team also learned early on the value of not giving up on a problem until it was completely solved. The problem they had was an excessive number of drums and pails in one of the production buildings. They collected data, came up with a solution and trained each of the crews on different shifts, but the problem still persisted. They investigated why and it turned out that everybody was not clear about what they were expected to do with the various drums and pails during the production process. Specifically, they did not know how to dispose of the containers and how to recycle product drawn off for sampling.

The team decided to show people exactly what was expected by making a 15-minute videotape. The videotape showed Jorge Lias (an hourly worker, team member and, coincidentally, the local union president) as he walked around the production area. He demonstrated the proper procedure by showing before and after scenarios. In the tape, he also showed how to dispose of drums and pails used in the process. This videotape, which was shown to everyone on the crews, was an excellent example of a team not letting go of a problem until they got back to the root cause.

As the first two teams became well established, two more teams were formed. One of these new teams was the energy management team which solved a problem with communication between members. This team had three bilingual (Spanish-English) people on it. However, one of these three could understand English as it was spoken, but was uncomfortable speaking it himself. Consequently, he was not participating in the meetings as much as was hoped. This was discovered as we did some team exercises to address issues of full participation, open and honest feedback, mutual support and listening skills.

In one exercise, we had each team member fill out a worksheet which had fifteen blank spaces after the names of different parts of a car. The team members were asked to put in the name of the person most like a certain car part. For example, the most forward-looking team member would be the headlights of a car; the person who was able to smooth out differences would be the springs.

The bilingual worker who was reluctant to speak English was identified as the luggage on top of the car. He was told that he was like a suitcase being taken on vacation — filled with good ideas, but difficult to get to or to get things out. The team then discussed with this individual that they valued his ideas and wanted him to participate more fully. They then brainstormed some possible solutions. They ended up deciding that the other two bilingual speakers would sit by this individual during meetings and translate whenever he needed it. He was told that he could ask for clarification at any time and that this was perfectly desirable. What was interesting was the fact that this person was smiling during the time when his problem was being discussed and solved. It turned out that he was more self-conscious about not being able to participate. He was happy because he had never realized until this exercise that the rest of the team liked his ideas.

Another team was able to make significant improvements by breaking a bottleneck in the process. The friction particle team is responsible for improving the processes that convert a product which includes pulverization. However, unless the pulverization can keep up with the chemical process back at the reactor vessel, it can slow down or halt production. This was precisely the area which the friction particle team was tasked to explore. They did just that by putting some measurements in place and by using problem solving techniques. The result four months later was a 54 percent increase in output. After breaking this bottleneck, the team was then anxious to look at other steps in the process in which they could increase output.

GENERAL FOODS
Dover, Delaware

Pro-Tech has been implementing a people involvement/empowerment program at this company for a number of years. We are happy to report that the people at this company still surprise us with their ingenuity and determination.

The first team we are going to discuss tackled a problem in General Foods' bundlekraft printing department. Bundlekraft is used as distribution packaging for Jell-O Brand as it comes off the production line. Bundlekraft comes in large master rolls which are run through a printing press where product data and bar codes are printed. The problem the company was experiencing was that they could not respond quickly enough to scheduling changes because of an excessive inventory of printed rolls (921 rolls which are 4 feet in diameter in the beginning), the running of large lot sizes, disruptions during printing and downtime in the production area.

The team attacked the problem by looking at the scheduling process and how they decide what's needed in production. They then looked at how they scheduled the supporting operation (bundlekraft printing) and, lastly, looked at issues surrounding machines and maintenance. The result of this activity was that the team was able to reduce the number of rolls in inventory to 356 (less than half!) in ten months. This was accomplished not by one change, but by a great number of small ones.

For example, the team saw that they were having a problem with bent cores which were made of paper. Normally, they were recycled back to the printer to be used again. Some would get damaged during handling. This resulted in not being able to mount the rolls on the packaging equipment. This problem was solved by following a flow chart of where the cores went, identifying the area where they got damaged and eliminating the root cause.

Part of the team's problem was solved when they obtained a third printing press from another plant. Now, two of the presses are permanently set up to run the two most popular widths of bundlekraft master rolls. This allowed them to eliminate a significant amount of set-up time normally associated with changing over from one product code to another. Now the set-up involves only changing printing plates. This will allow them to reduce inventory and cycle time even further.

Another team at General Foods, the cycle counting team, was attempting to improve inventory record accuracy. One of the first obstacles they overcame was scheduling team meetings since the team is made up of third and first shift personnel. Since the end of the third shift and beginning of the first was at 7 a.m., the team elected to meet from 6:30 - 7:30 a.m. That done, the team decided to use control group counting to identify systemic errors more quickly. They picked 100 items which constituted a good cross-section of the inventory and counted them once a week. Their measure was the percentage of product codes with no error at all in the control group.

For those items which were not accurate, the team used Pareto analysis to identify not only the root causes, but the leading root causes which were eliminated one at a time. Even though all material issues continued to be keypunched once a day from sheets manually prepared by forklift operators, the team was able to achieve 96 percent record accuracy within the control group. Overall inventory accuracy reached 94 percent. General Foods is implementing a bar coding system to reach the next level of accuracy.

Yet another team at General Foods attacked the problem of service to internal customers. The warehouse servicing team began looking at servicing errors to the production department. The team used Deming's philosophy that 85 percent of all errors are the result of the management system. Therefore, when they went looking for root causes, they did not focus on individual forklift drivers, but on why there were errors. It turned out that a great number of errors were the result of drivers needing to write down transactions on a crowded form which did not allow enough room for individual handwriting styles. While the team realized that the long-term solution was to eliminate the need for handwriting, short-term benefits were obtained by redesigning the form.

The warehouse maintenance team's charter stated that this team would look at the palletizing of product as it came off an automated production line. By measuring downtime, the team found that a portion of the downtime had nothing to do with the palletizer, but with the conveyors that led from the production line to the warehouse. The team discovered that after some cleaning operations, switches for electric eyes were left on or off and were blocking the smooth flow of product. Further investigation revealed that the training program for people doing the cleaning operations was inadequate. The training program was changed to include instruction in what switches to leave on and turn off.

General Foods also formed a sanitation council, a plant-wide committee whose purpose was to address the extremely important sanitation issues in this industry. The council was set up like a steering committee. It met once a month and oversaw the activities of sanitation people involvement/empowerment teams in each department. All of these teams met once a week to achieve zero contamination. As a result of their efforts, General Foods was recently awarded an "excellent" audit status by the American Institute of Baking.

The company also addressed employee training in the "three R's" on a plant-wide scale. We had conducted a needs assessment when we began consulting at General Foods and discovered (as is typical of many American companies) a great need for training in reading, writing and arithmetic skills. The company responded to this need by developing a computer-based, in-house training center to diagnose and train people.

The goal of training and other people involvement/empowerment activities is to create self-directed work teams which will handle all issues around the Continuous Improvement Process. Several production areas have already eliminated the need for supervisors and operate with a team manager in the department, but with no supervisory level between that person and the team members.

We always like to bring up the example of one individual at General Foods who started as a total non-believer and has now become our greatest proponent. It shows what a company can do when it respects the needs of its people. We were conducting a training program in set-up reduction at the plant — two days of education for the program's steering committee and upper management, two days for set-up reduction team members and four hours for the remaining employees at the facility. Our goal was not to have anybody say "What is set-up reduction?" when we were finished.

In one of the employee sessions, we were about two hours or so into the presentation when we noticed that two key set-up people (one from the day shift and one from the night) were in the back of the room whispering to each other. We asked them if there was a problem.

One of them stood up and told us in no uncertain terms what he thought about the program and what we could do with it. He also told us that he was going to leave the meeting.

We asked him why.

"I'm sick and tired of experts coming in," he said, "and telling us that we've been messing up all these years."

Fine, we told him. We need you to be a part of this program, but if you feel you have to leave, then go ahead. And *both* of them left. After the session, we went to the employee's supervisor and said, "We would like to talk to this man in the conference room tomorrow at 8 a.m. for two hours."

The next morning, we got there early and set up a flip chart and put a chair in front of it. When our friend came in, we said, "Please sit down. For the next two hours, this is what we are going to do. For the first forty minutes, you will listen to us go through set-up reduction one more time. Then you will tell us your ideas about how to help the company's competitive posture."

We went through our presentation and asked him for his ideas.

"I don't have any ideas," he told us. "My only concern is that I've been doing changeovers for thirty-three years and I don't want you to make me look stupid."

We told him that we understood his feelings and then asked him if others felt the same way.

"A lot," he told us.

Thanks to this employee, we were alerted to a very important issue that we knew the company had to address before it could move forward with its implementation. The problem, in fact, centered around the issue of videotaping employees while they performed a set-up. Many of them were understandably concerned that these tapes would be used against them during job reviews. We had to assure them that this was not the purpose. The consensus was that we were going to use the videotapes to make the workers look stupid, which could not be further from the truth.

The way we cleared this hurdle was to address their fears squarely. We told the set-up people that we would make a videotape of them doing a changeover. We would then give the tape to them for three weeks to watch. They could study it by themselves and make whatever improvements they wanted to in the way they did the changeover. After those three weeks, we would videotape them again as they performed a changeover. When we were finished, we would give them the tape and tell them that they had to bring it to the next team meeting.

At the team meetings, the members and the set-up person would review the tape, using the changeover reduction process (discussed in our book, **Set-Up Reduction: Saving Dollars with Common Sense**, PT Publications, Palm Beach Gardens, FL) and look for ways to reduce set-up time. After the meeting, the set-up person could bring the tape home on the condition that he brought it back to the next meeting. When the team decided that the tape was no longer representative of the changeover (because of improvements), then a new videotape would be made and the old videotape destroyed. This was how we assured the workers that the videotapes would not be used for job reviews.

CAVAL TOOL
Newington, Connecticut

This high-tech company wanted to use a people involvement/ empowerment program as part of their strategic positioning and planning program for the future. Under the umbrellas of Total Quality Management, Pro-Tech is helping Caval Tool become a World Class company poised to leap into the twenty-first century.

Caval Tool machines complex components for the aerospace and satellite industries. Aerospace is an industry undergoing tremendous change, including a reduction in sales. Despite this, TQM and people involvement/empowerment has enabled Caval to maintain business and even grow into new areas. The two largest customers of this 220-employee company recently recognized Caval as being "light-years" ahead of its competition in terms of Total Quality Management (TQM) and people involvement/ empowerment. All of the hardships in the industry make Caval's story even more remarkable.

Elmer Miller, vice president of operations and general manager, decided that the only way for Caval to meet its strategic objectives was to embark upon a plan of people involvement with a long-term goal of people empowerment. The intent was to begin with cross-functional teams and then to develop self-directed work teams as well when people involvement/empowerment took hold. All of these activities were done under the umbrella of TQM, so the first step was to form a steering committee to implement Total Quality and Statistical Process Control (SPC). The steering committee was co-chaired by Marty Regan, quality manager, and Eileen Morris, personnel manager, who were elected by consensus. One other important person was the TQM coordinator, Steve Ferraro, who was selected by Miller and appointed full-time to the position. This full-time appointment is significant in light of the fact that Caval runs "lean and mean." The person was an hourly worker from the quality department who was vocal about the need for change and knowledgeable about Total Quality. An hourly worker was purposely chosen in order to reinforce the bottom-up approach of people involvement/empowerment.

The steering committee met twice a month for one and a half hours each time. Its purpose was to draft policy and monitor the people involvement/empowerment program. Initially, we helped the committee develop a mission statement and draw up an implementation plan, but when the program started, it was expected that the steering committee and the TQM coordinator would take ownership.

The program began with everybody getting a two-hour general awareness training session in people involvement/empowerment. We not only talked about the principles behind this philosophy but why Caval was moving into this area. The reason for the company's move was simple to explain. Caval felt that it was underutilizing its employees and wouldn't be able to meet its strategic objectives without drawing on this invaluable resource. At this session, we also talked about what was going on elsewhere in American industry and what other companies were doing in response to the business challenges of the future. We used many examples from our work at other clients to discuss and justify the need for people involvement/empowerment.

A week after the training sessions, we did an attitude survey of all the employees on their thoughts about TQM and the new process. The feedback was very encouraging and supportive. Understandably, there was some doubt best expressed as "Is management really going to go through with this?" We shared the results with the employees and the steering committee which wanted to know what needed to be done to convince employees that change was really going to happen. As we found out, the steering committee was particularly sensitive to any issues focusing on employee reluctance. A sizable portion of the work force, like most companies, were rightfully suspicious of "five-year plans" of any sort. (We call this phenomenon, "flavor of the month" management.) We are happy to say that these issues were all successfully encountered and we got more volunteers than was needed for the first two waves of teams. Again, we saw the value of addressing an issue head-on.

First Wave of Teams

The first four teams chosen by the steering committee based their decision on where they could get the most payback. The four teams were:

1. **Set-up Reduction** — Its purpose was to break the economics of lot sizing so they could control work-in-process and thus reduce lead-time to customers while increasing responsiveness.

2. **Gauging** — This team's area of concern was ensuring consistency of results between operator inspection and quality inspection. In addition, it was tasked with the need to establish the repeatability and reproducibility standards required for SPC.

3. **Outside Services** — This team's responsibility was to work on supplier quality and on-time delivery.

4. **Visual Defects** — This team's task was to address the high percentage of rework related to visual defects and the emotionally charged environment between Quality and Production as a result of these defects.

Extensive training of the teams was followed by charter development meetings which the steering committee adopted with minimal changes. With the charter in place, each team brainstormed their fishbone chart and developed measurements which would allow them to fulfill their charter.

Pro-Tech conducted the first three meetings for each team. At the third meeting, the teams elected their own leaders. We worked with this individual in a transition period where the leader received three two-hour training sessions which included the role of a team leader, how to conduct meetings, build consensus and how to deal with interpersonal issues. We also stressed keeping an eye on attendance and encouraging equal participation. Everyone on a team would be expected to take an action item at every meeting. It was important as well, we told the new leaders, to publish the agenda before each meeting and to follow it. During this period of training, the team also elected team scribes and we conducted a two-hour training session for them.

As needed, each team received topic-specific training. For example, the set-up reduction team chose a short course in quick changeover techniques. In this course, they were given two case studies in which they analyzed videotapes of set-ups. The second case study was a videotape of a set-up at Caval and it subsequently became the team's first project which ended very successfully. The team recommended some workplace reorganization and projected first year savings of $7,200 for changes costing $1,200. A few months later, the same ideas were used in another department and projected savings there were $39,000 at a cost of $1,700.

Earlier, we mentioned the importance of attendance at team meetings. This issue always comes up in people involvement/ empowerment programs. We dealt with the problem at Caval by addressing it up front. In our initial training sessions, we had teams practice brainstorming techniques. The topic which they were to brainstorm was why people are late for meetings. Their ideas were used later when the team set ground rules to prevent tardiness and absenteeism.

A typical rule to come out of one of these practice sessions was to let the supervisor know in advance when the employee had to attend a meeting. In addition, the team asked each member to share what went on at meetings with their supervisors and fellow workers in order to curry support and enthusiasm. If there is a legitimate reason for not attending, the teams decided that the member would need to alert the team leader ahead of time and still complete his action item on time.

The following example gives you some idea of what is not a legitimate reason for missing a meeting and how the situation can be resolved. Early in the implementation, there was a situation where a "hot" part had to be sent out of the plant that day. The team member told the team leader in the morning that he would not be able to attend the meeting. The team leader tried to work something out with the member's supervisor, but was unable to find a common solution. At this point, we got involved since we saw the situation as an opportunity to show top management support.

Elmer Miller called the supervisor on the phone and tried to work out a way to ship the part and allow the team member to attend the meeting. Eventually, the supervisor was able to find an operator in an adjoining department qualified to run the machine during the hour that the team member was away. Here again is proof that we can solve problems if we put our heads together to satisfy the needs of teams and customers.

Second Wave of Teams

Four months after the first wave of teams, Caval put together the four all-volunteer teams which follow:

1. **Paperwork Reduction** — This team was given the opportunity to eliminate or reduce paperwork in any and all departments of the company. The team also has a representative from one of their external customers to help look at issues between Caval and the customer.

2. **Suggestion/Communication** — This team's charter instructed them to look at communication in the company and to help transition out the old "pay for suggestion" practice for one encouraging suggestions as part of everyone's job, not just those looking for extra income. The team was seeking to eliminate the phenomena where 80 percent of the suggestions come from only 20 percent of the people.

3. **Queue Reduction** — Actually, this team could be called the Increased Throughput team because its task was to find ways to reduce cycle time from

engineering release through customer delivery to
accounts receivable. This team overlaps to some
extent with the Set-Up Reduction team.

4. **Equipment** — This team was working on improving equipment effectiveness by addressing maintenance and capability issues.

Another problem that often occurs on teams is when a member
fails to complete an action item on time. This happened at Caval
and we are proud to say that our training in team development
helped one team solve the problem quite nicely. The team first
attempted to address the problem in a supportive manner with the
individual at a team meeting. When that failed to solve the
problem of incomplete action items, the team leader met one-on-
one with the person. During that encounter, the team leader
discovered that the individual did not have enough time during the
work week to complete the one hour required for the action item.
The team leader then set up a three-way meeting with the person's
supervisor to enlist his support in helping the individual find time.

At that meeting, it turned out that the real problem was not time,
but that the individual was intimidated by some of the math
required to complete performance charts. Now that the problem
had been truly identified, the team leader worked out a plan
whereby he would work with the individual on his action items
until he was confident enough to complete them by himself. The
key point in this example was getting the supervisor involved and
to do it in a supportive, positive manner in which we look for root
causes and not to blame individuals.

This particular problem came to the attention of the steering
committee who recognized that a number of other people in the

company faced the same problem as the individual discussed above. Caval is now working with the State of Connecticut to obtain a grant to help pay for remedial training under a program designed to help keep jobs in the state. There are similar programs in many states. Some of our other clients have taken advantage of them as well.

Program Assessment

While working with Caval, we also conducted a program assessment which highlighted areas of concern for the company in the future. There are two areas on which the company is currently working:

---

1. **Not enough emphasis being placed on identifying and satisfying both internal and external customers.**

2. **Changing the way teams are picked from being done by the consensus of the steering committee to being driven by employees identifying areas of opportunity based on overall TQM measurements and analyses.**

One steering committee member, John Obara, engineering manager, couldn't wait to get his people involved in the first of these areas. He informally addressed the issue by setting out to satisfy one of his department's internal customers, manufacturing. As is typical of many companies, the two departments over the years had communication problems, but John and some of his engineers decided to change that by talking with some of their customers, the foremen and operators on the floor, about how they would rate

Engineering as a supplier. The outgrowth of these discussions was a checklist for Manufacturing to use in assessing how accurate, complete and on-time each release of an engineering package was from their department.

As for the second area, Caval wanted to make sure members of the steering committee were as close to the production process as possible to steer it effectively, but not so close as to stifle innovation. They opted to accept our proposal to begin a mentoring program at the company. The program worked in this way: Each team had a member of the steering committee as its team mentor. The mentor's job was to keep in touch with the team in a non-technical, supportive manner. He or she was supposed to attend one team meeting a month by invitation only; to make personal contact with each team member twice a month; and to contact the team leader once a week.

These contacts were primarily informal, but allowed team members to give feedback directly to the steering committee about any concerns they may have had regarding the people involvement/ empowerment process. It also, of course, made sure that steering committee members stayed close to the process as well.

Although we think highly of the mentoring program, it is a process in itself which needs to be monitored carefully. It can be all too easy for a mentor to get involved in details and all too easy for a team to start relying too heavily on the mentor. We always tell teams that it is permissible to go outside for assistance if the expertise is not on the team, but that the mentor should not provide that kind of support. His or her support should be morale boosting during tough times. In fact, one mentor at Caval was unfortunately assigned to a team dealing with a problem in which he was an expert. He started attending every meeting and participating like a team member. We advised the team either to make him a member or to limit his mentoring to what is described above. To allow him to help in this manner, although useful in the short term, would stifle the team's effectiveness in the long term. On the other hand, a mentor should not take the attitude that if the team needs him or her, then they should come looking for him. The team mentor must be actively involved, without being controlling.

BIBLIOGRAPHY

Fortune, Marshall Loeb, Editor; James B. Hayes, Publisher; New York, NY.

The Improvement Book: *Creating the Problem-free Workplace*, Tomo Sugiyama; Productivity Press, Cambridge, MA, 1989.

People: *Managing Your Most Important Asset*, Harvard Business Review, Boston, MA, 1986.

Change Agents, Manuel London; Josey-Bass Publishers, San Francisco, CA, 1988.

Small Group Communication in Organizations, H. Lloyd Goodall, Jr.; Wm. C. Brown Publishers, Dubuque, IA, 1985.

The Human Side of Enterprise, Douglas M. McGregor; McGraw-Hill, New York, NY, 1985.

Theory Z, William G. Ouchi; Addison-Wesley, Reading, MA, 1981.

Set-Up Reduction: *Saving Dollars with Common Sense*, Jerry W. Claunch and Philip D. Stang; PT Publications, Palm Beach Gardens, FL, 1989.

Team Development Manual, Mike Woodcock; Gower Publishing, Brookfield, VT, 1989.

Creating Excellence: *Managing Corporate Culture, Strategy and Change in the New Age*, Craig R. Hickman and Michael A. Silva; New American Library, New York, NY, 1984.

Wall Street Journal, Robert Bartley, Editor; Peter R. Kann, Publisher, New York, NY.

Change Masters, Rosabeth Moss Kanter; Simon & Schuster, New York, NY, 1983.

Team Building, Wayne G. Dyer; Addison-Wesley, Reading, MA, 1987.

Teamwork: *Involving People in Quality and Productivity Improvement*, Charles A. Aubrey, II and Patricia K. Felkins; Quality Press, Milwaukee, WI, 1988.

Attitude: *Your Most Priceless Possession*, Elwood N. Chapman; Crisp Publications, Los Altos, CA, 1987.

Love and Profit, James A. Autry; Morrow, New York, NY, 1991.

Harvard Business Review, Theodore Levitt, Editor; James A. McGowan, Publisher, Boston, MA.

Industry Week, Charles R. Day, Jr., Editor; Vincent A. Castell, Publisher, Cleveland, OH.

Managing Automation, Robert Malone, Editor; Ralph E. Richardson, Publisher, New York, NY.

USA Today, John C. Quinn, Editor; Cathleen Black, Publisher, Washington, DC.

Made In America: *The Total Business Concept*, Peter L. Grieco, Jr. and Michael W. Gozzo; PT Publications, Palm Beach Gardens, FL, 1987.

World Class: *Measuring Its Achievement*, Peter L. Grieco, Jr.; PT Publications, Palm Beach Gardens, FL, 1990.

Behind Bars: *Bar Coding Principles and Applications*, Peter L. Grieco, Jr., Michael W. Gozzo, C.J. (Chip) Long; PT Publications, Palm Beach Gardens, FL, 1989.

Just-In-Time Purchasing: *In Pursuit of Excellence*, Peter L. Grieco, Jr., Michael W. Gozzo, Jerry W. Claunch; PT Publications, Palm Beach Gardens, FL, 1988.

The World of Negotiations: *Never Being a Loser*, Peter L. Grieco, Jr. and Paul G. Hine; PT Publications, Palm Beach Gardens, FL, 1991.

Supplier Certification: *Achieving Excellence*, Peter L. Grieco, Jr., Michael W. Gozzo, Jerry W. Claunch; PT Publications, Palm Beach Gardens, FL, 1988.

APPENDIX A: HOW TO HAVE PRODUCTIVE MEETINGS

This appendix gives you an overview of the rules and skills required to have successful and productive meetings. It should be emphasized that the key to such a meeting is the employment of the principles of the Continuous Improvement Process to the meeting itself. In other words, each meeting should teach members something about how to run the next meeting even more effectively.

LAYING THE GROUNDWORK

- **Employ agendas.** Team members should have a road map of where the meeting is headed as far in advance as possible. Agendas should include topics of discussion, the people initiating discussion or giving reports and the estimated amount of time each topic shall take.

- **Use a team leader/facilitator.** This person's critical role is to keep meetings focused and moving in a productive direction.

- **Designate a scribe or a policy for selecting a scribe.** A scribe should record key subjects discussed and points made for and against, as well as decisions reached by the team.

- **Allow no interruptions.** One rule that some use: If you were 100 miles away, would you leave the meeting to solve this problem?

- **Plan the next meeting.** Discuss and draw up an agenda for the next meeting.

- **Leave time for evaluation.** Team members should discuss how they can improve the meeting process.

LEARNING THE NECESSARY TEAM SKILLS

Both the team leader/facilitator and team members should pay attention to these skills.

- **Question what you don't know.** If a team member is unclear about an area, encourage him or her to get clarification or ask the speaker to explain the area in another way.

- **Ensure equal participation.** The team leader/facilitator should not allow one person or faction to dominate.

- **Sum up what has been discussed.** Every now and then, the team leader/facilitator should summarize the proceedings of the meeting to make sure that everybody is "on the same wavelength" and in consensus.

- **Keep an eye on the clock.** The team leader/ facilitator should warn speakers when their time is about to run out and, conversely, open up discussion if more time is required.

- **Know when to end the meeting.** The team leader/facilitator should look for moments when further discussion only leads to paralysis and then move the group on to the next topic.

KEEPING THE RECORD BOOKS

It is vital for teams to maintain up-to-date and accurate records of their discussions, actions and results. Not only will this help the team keep on track, but it will help future teams copy their successes and improve upon them.

- **Save those agendas.** Agendas will give you, or future teams, a quick overview of what got done and when.

- **Save those minutes.** Team minutes are just as important as agendas. Make sure the team has kept a list of what action was decided upon and who agreed to undertake the task. Also, be sure to list those items which will require future action.

- **Save those results.** Results are the reward
  for a job well done, but they are also
  justification for expanding people
  involvement/empowerment programs
  throughout the company in order to
  continue the improvement process.

SETTING GOALS FOR THE FIRST FEW MEETINGS

The goals of the first few meetings center around two topics:
Team building goals and educational goals. Don't hesitate to
spend two or more meetings on these topics before you even
begin to discuss problems if the members have never been on a
team before.

Team Building Goals

- **Learn about each other's background.**

- **Find ways to use each other's strengths and
  compensate for each other's weaknesses.**

- **Decide how the team will make a decision —
  by majority vote, two-thirds rule, consensus, etc.**

- **Locate resources and determine channels for
  using them.**

- **Discuss rules for missed meetings, tardiness,
  meeting place and time and other
  procedural matters.**

Educational Goals

- **Discuss the Continuous Improvement Process (CIP) and how teams and employee involvement/empowerment programs are used to further company goals.**

- **Learn problem solving and information-gathering skills as discussed in Chapter 6.**

By following the guidelines above, you will save time, effort and money in the long run. These rules and skills provide a very solid base upon which any employee involvement/empowerment program is sure to grow to fruition.

APPENDIX B:
SAMPLE TEAM PRESENTATIONS

The purpose of team presentations is to provide communication to the steering committee, to build self-confidence in team members and to gain company-wide support. We recommend that team presentations be done on a quarterly basis. The presentation itself should be between 15 and 20 minutes long and contain an agenda and other related material, if necessary, to hand out.

Data for the presentation primarily comes from the minutes of team meetings and from performance measurements put into place to measure the team's activities. We also highly recommend that everybody on the team be given some piece of the presentation to work on. You should strive for total participation. Lastly, it is a good idea to do a dry run, or rehearsal, in order to work out any kinks.

The presentations from our clients on the following pages illustrate what we mean.

SAMPLE 1   **[Page 1]**

P • R • I • D • E

Price Reduction Including Delivery
Excellence

Participants:
Mike Branch
Richard Chaillaux
Tom DeFranco
Nick Farana
Gary Prentice

[Page 2]

MISSION STATEMENT

To selectively reduce material costs
and improve overall quality and
delivery performance.

[Page 3]

I. PROBLEMS DEFINED AND RESOLVED:

Connectors by Gary Prentice

Printed Circuits by Tom DeFranco

Sheetmetal Inspection by Mike Branch

II. NEW ACTIVITIES:

Rack Mount Kit by Nick Farana

60" Enclosures (disk/system cabinet) by Nick Farana

CONNECTORS

PROBLEM: *The connector in both male and female versions had a rejection rate in excess of 25% in calendar year 1990. For a time, they were incapable of delivering any product.*

WHY?: *The supplier had process problems causing multiple inconsistencies to the specifications for those parts.*

SOLUTION: *Identify problems via fishbone analysis and meet with supplier to review and correct.*

OVERALL TOOLING PROBLEMS CAUSING:

> — *Misalignment of terminals*
> — *Insufficient/Inconsistent solder*
> — *Male pin burrs*

SAVINGS: *Hours avoided in 1991 is 510 which is equal to $16,000 and 0% rejection rate achieved.*

[Page 5]

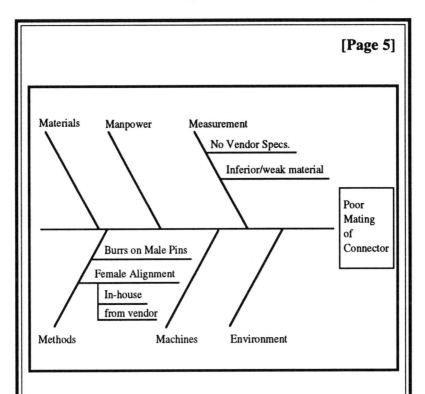

[Page 6]

PRINTED CIRCUITS

PROBLEM: *The number of printed circuits and printed circuit lots had reached unacceptable rejection levels in 1990.*

SCOPE: *All Server 8000 printed circuit boards.*

SOLUTION: *REJECTS — Supplier adds In-Process Quality Control check points and final audit on PCBs prior to shipment.*
LATE DELIVERIES — Adds an interim step as a two-week buffer in their production cycle to account for less than 100% yields and guarantee on-time delivery.

COSTS: *None to ShareBase.*

SAVINGS: *Elimination of rework to rejected PCBs that could not be returned to vendor due to schedule constraints.*

Rwk. labor @ $50.00 per PCB X 16 PCBs = $800.00

A significant number of PCBs will no longer require premium time for their assembly to get back on production schedule.

Prem/labor @ $38.00 per PCB X 50 PCBs =
$1900.00

Total savings = $2700.00

SHEETMETAL INSPECTION

PROBLEM: *To eliminate redundant incoming inspection for fabricated parts (i.e. sheetmetal) ordered on blanket agreements where the vendor opts to fabricate more than one delivery and up to ninety days production.*

SCOPE: *Incoming Q.A. and Stockroom.*

SOLUTION: *Inspect only the initial release of the blanket order since subsequent deliveries against a given order will have been processed at the same time and would therefore not have characteristics unique from the initially inspected lot. Establish a procedure called LOT INSPECTION APPROVAL PROGRAM (L.I.A.P.) to meet this goal and provide necessary assurances of vendor conformance.*

SAVINGS: *Reduction of incoming Q.A. time on sheetmetal results in an estimated 52.2 hours, at a burden rate of $21.92 per hour for an average annual savings of $4,576.88.*

By reducing the incoming Q.A., we also reduce the material lead time by one week (the time eliminated by L.I.A.P. formerly required for inspection of sheetmetal parts). This will result in an additional savings of $736.00.

[Page 8]

NEW PROJECTS

1. Replacement of Rack Mount Kit for peripherals installed in cabinets currently purchased from Seagate with one fabricated by a ShareBase fabricator. This is a two-phase project: 1) Copy the current version as it is, reducing the unit cost by $50.00 per unit over 200 units annually saving $10,000 and 2) Taking it a step further and have the Rack Mount Kit redesigned by our M.E. for a further saving of $40.00 per unit (approx.) for another $8000.00 per year.

2. Simplify design of 60" disk/system cabinet to achieve $150.00 per cabinet reduction over 150 units for $12,500.00 annual savings.

I. nventory

R. eduction

S. ociety

THE **I.R.S.** WILL STRIVE TO CONTINUALLY RE-
DUCE AND BETTER MANAGE OUR INVENTORIES
THROUGH A TEAM EFFORT, ENABLING LORAN TO
PROVIDE CUSTOMERS THE HIGHEST QUALITY
PRODUCT, BECOME MORE PROFITABLE, COM-
PETITIVE AND ESTABLISH A HOME AMONGST THE
LEADERS IN THE AUDIO MARKETPLACE.

We, The I.R.S. Team . . .

Randy Britton - Leader	**Cathy Solock**
Amy Mangini - Scribe	**Wanda Vincent**
Scott Korchak	**Tami Case**
Kelly Leofsky	**Greg Leofsky**
Nancy Saber	**Sally Strain**

. . . would like to welcome the
Steering Committee to our presentation.

The Agenda is as follows:

1. Introduction of members.

2. Where did we begin?

3. Our Accomplishments.

4. Where are we now?

5. Where are we going?

6. Question and Answer period.

Where did we start?

*   1st meeting - 12/5/89
      — Elected Team Leader & Scribe. (Randy/Amy)
      — Initial assignments were made with the assistance of
        Pro-Tech consultant.

*   Consensus made on Team Name: IRS (Inventory
      Reduction Society)

**   **ENTHUSIASM WAS VERY HIGH AT THIS POINT
      TO GET MOVING **

*   Consensus made on Mission Statement:

      —   The I R S will strive to continually reduce and
            better manage our inventories through a team effort,
            enabling LORAN to provide customers the highest
            quality product, become more profitable, competi-
            tive and establish a home amongst the leaders in the
            audio marketplace.

*   With the help of Pro-Tech, we set our initial goal and
      established a timeframe to accomplish it:

      —   50% reduction by 7/11/90
            (Initial inventory = $326,714)
            (Goal would be = $163,357)

      —   60% of that should be met by 3/11/90

      —   80% of that total by 5/11/90

*   Today's inventory $'s: $184,029

*   Brainstormed Causes of Inventory.

     — Fishbone diagram.

*   Initial Assignment of bar graphing ALL Inventory
     (Raw Mtl, WIP, FG) directed the team to attack Raw
     Material as it contained the highest $ amount. ($278,474)

*   Pareto Chart created by Raw Material Item classes
     directed us to focus on top (3) item classes w/ the highest
     $ amounts which are as follows:

     1 JAL Assembly Components

     2 JBL Packout Components

     3 Miscellaneous Raw Materials

                                                 [Page 4]

*   Began to struggle somewhat, mainly due to lack of
     direction on everyone's part. It was here that we started
     to take on new tasks without completing the initial ones.
     Again, this was due to lack of direction and we didn't
     know where to go. In light of this, we saw no results and
     frustration set in.

*   With the help of problem-solving training and also
     facilitation by Pro-Tech, we began getting back on track.

*   Going back to initial brainstorming/fishbone charts and began attacking the obsolete inactive inventory beginning with the JAL components.

*   Also playing a large role in assisting reduction of inventories is the Purchasing and Production Control Depts. Large portions of our reduction stem from smaller lot sizes and more frequent deliveries.

      — Purchasing should be commended for their efforts!

[Page 5]

PROJECT INVENTORY REDUCTION

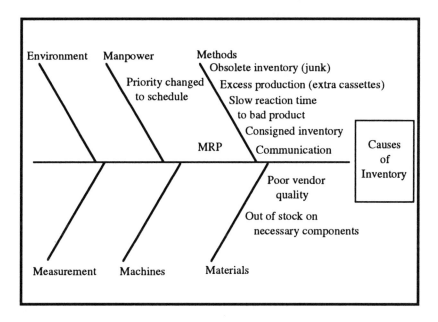

[Page 6]

IRS TEAM
ACCOMPLISHMENTS

*　　Consensus on team name, logo, and mission statement.

*　　Completed 12 hours of inventory training and 4 hours of
　　MRP. (better understanding of how to achieve our goals)

*　　Posting of monthly inventory numbers on employee
　　bulletin board.

*　　Reduced inactive inventory by $9421.40.

　　• Approval received to use:
　　　　Hubs (white and black)
　　　　Idlers (white and black)
　　• Approval received to scrap clear bikini slip sheets

*　　Reached our original goal for 50% reduction in
　　inventory $'s.

*　　We are holding more productive and focused meetings.

LORAN INVENTORIES
Breakdown

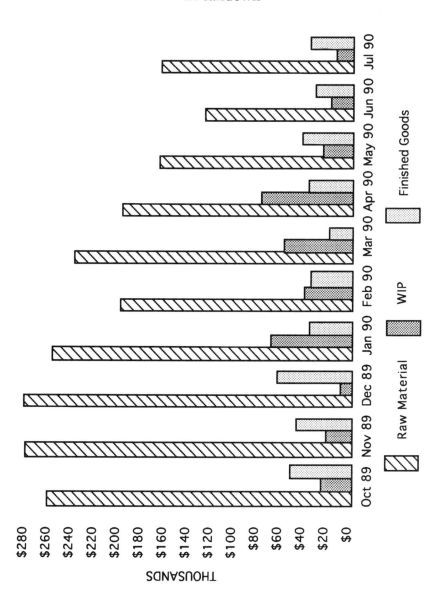

INDEX